First Time Ironman

Dedication

For Laura, my love and inspiration
For Eva-Rose, my beautiful daughter
To God for being with me always

FIRST TIME
IRONMAN

RHYS CHONG

ecademyPRESS
www.ecademy-press.com

First Time Ironman

First published in 2012 by

Ecademy Press
48 St Vincent Drive, St Albans, Herts, AL1 5SJ
info@ecademy-press.com
www.ecademy-press.com

Printed and bound by Lightning Source in the UK and USA
Photography by Michael Inns
Artwork by Karen Gladwell

Printed on acid-free paper from managed forests.
This book is printed on demand, so no copies will
be remaindered or pulped.

ISBN 978-1-907722-99-8

Contents

Acknowledgements

Ironman coaching team

Fran Campana, Emile Bitar, Dave Taylor, Chris Janzen, Michelle Pollard, Sonja Fairfield, Dr Justin Roberts.

Support team at the race

Laura Chong, Fran Campana, Bruce & Monique Scott, Bruce & Michelle Goldfinch, Debbie & Tony Lucas, Joel Lucas.

Worldwide team

Evelyn & Billy Chong, Justin & Rachel Chong, Vicki & Matt Lahana and all my friends in London who encouraged me and donated generously to my nominated charity KIVA.

Publishing

Mindy Gibbins-Klein and Team at The Book Midwife Michael Inns and Karen Gladwell for design, artwork and PR photography.

Debbie Lucas for proof reading.

"As a first time Ironman and half way through my Ironman programme I am glad I read Rhys' experience. I have been training for 3 months so far, 6 days a week and started to feel the training getting to me. Having read what Rhys went through, gave me confidence to keep at it, even with the setbacks I started to have. It was exactly what I have been experiencing through my journey thus far. I would definitely recommend reading this book to anyone starting their Ironman journey, it is an easy read and full of very useful information

Senan Haddad - *First Time Ironman Triathlete*

Introduction

This book was written after I completed my first Ironman in Switzerland. The Ironman was the greatest physical challenge I wanted to complete in my lifetime. For 10 years I had fooled myself into believing I could never do one.

It was having the guts to confront my fears and prepare for the unknown, which started this incredible journey. I trained consistently for one year and worked with a team of experienced professionals to eventually enjoy the sweet success of crossing that finish line.

I wanted to share this journey with you so first-time Ironman athletes could get a preview of what training and racing an Ironman is like, the highs and the lows. The book is divided into chapters, which run in chronological order from the start of my journey to post Ironman recovery. Each chapter contains stories of my personal experiences and ends with my 3 Top Tips to take away.

The Ironman changed my life because through the training I learned how to optimise my nutrition, build an athletic body and set and achieve unthinkable goals. It deepened my personal relationships and I now support a charity on a regular basis. The Ironman has become a part of my identity and I use it to push myself through life's challenges and onto greater levels of enjoyment. Completing an Ironman is more than completing a race. When you cross the finish line you will know just how much it means.

Every Ironman's journey is unique and inspirational. It is my honour to share my journey with you and I hope it inspires more men and women to become first-time Ironman athletes.

Foreword

"I could NEVER do that!"

Those were the words that I often repeated as a teenager as I spent a lazy autumn afternoon on the couch watching ABC's Wide World of Sports coverage of the Hawaii Ironman Triathlon.

To me those athletes – led by legends Dave Scott and Mark Allen – were superhuman and from another planet. Seriously.

How is it possible for someone to race in that heat, at that pace, for that long? Surely they were simply 'born extra talented', a genetically gifted species that the average human simply could not relate to, nor truly understand.

And even for those, like myself, already athletically inclined and very physically active, the task seemed too impossible, too daunting and too ridiculous to ever consider.

Or was it?

As a young athlete growing up in Canada in the 80's I had no fear on the football field, hockey rink or basketball court. I always felt blessed to have very good hand-eye coordination, which lent itself very well to most of the team sports I played. A natural talent combined with a lot of practice and a healthy dose of ambition, continued to fuel me to compete and push myself to a new level every season. Many of those seasons ended with winning championships and the honour of being named the most valuable player.

So I had every reason to be confident in my abilities as an athlete.

Yet as I watched those men and women compete in the blazing sun around the lava fields of Hawaii, I remained in awe. I could never do that. Too hard, too impossible, too much time needed to train, train, train!

Since then, in the 20+ years gone by, I learned a lot of what it takes to achieve the impossible and that a vast capacity – physically, emotionally, mentally and spiritually – lies within each and every one of us to face enormous challenges, overcome incredible odds and achieve amazing things. Especially things that we used to believe could never happen to us.

In this book, Rhys sheds valuable light on the real experience of becoming an Ironman. Well before the glory and tears (and searing pain in the legs) that every first time Ironman expects at the finishing line, there is work to be done.

Rhys not only tells it like it is but outlines the necessary ingredients to make your Ironman journey a healthy, happy and memorable experience. Whether you're a busy business owner or a busier family man or woman, you can have a life and attempt the Ironman as Rhys clearly demonstrates. From proper coaching and training plans to managing your mind and your time, any aspiring Ironman will find his advice comforting and inspiring.

Rhys inspired me as well.

I may not have even started to train for an Ironman if it wasn't for my in-depth and personal involvement as Rhys' Mental Conditioning Coach. The opportunity to get inside his mind, understand his fears and share in the rush of adrenaline as he climbed The Beast and made his dream a reality, stirred something inside me and reignited my fire to set big goals.

On November 27, 2011, I achieved my own 'impossible' when I crossed the finish line at Ironman Cozumel. 13 hours, 2 minutes and 16 seconds of pure fun, pain, frustration and joy.

I hope this book stirs something inside you too and I encourage you to go boldly forward, to dream big and never, ever forget that you can always do more than you think you can.

To your potential and exceeding your own expectations,

Chris Janzen

Founder of TriathleteMind.com & Inner Game Coach
Proud Ironman Finisher

CHAPTER ONE

The 10 year decision

The decision to enter an Ironman sparked a cascade of events that would end in one of the most rewarding experiences of my life. Finishing the Ironman – a 2.4-mile (3.86 kilometre) swim, a 112-mile (180.25 kilometre) bike ride and a marathon (26.2 miles or 42.195 kilometres) – in one day was a testimony to one year of careful planning and disciplined training. The physical and emotional experience along this incredible journey was unparalleled to anything I had ever achieved before.

For 10 years the thought of doing an Ironman had sat in the back of my mind. I had completed a Half Ironman in New Zealand 10 years ago and promised myself I would complete the full Ironman once in my lifetime. The Half Ironman was a tough race and afterwards I lost the desire to train again. I left New Zealand to live in London and thought my Ironman dream was over. My life in London seemed too busy and it was too dark and cold in winter to even consider training for an Ironman.

My Ironman dream was suddenly reignited 10 years after arriving in London. I started working in a gym in Fulham, as a physiotherapist. In this gym were two personal trainers who lived and breathed Ironman. One was a professional Ironman athlete and the other had completed five Ironman races as an amateur. I saw them train in the gym, bring in their Tri bikes, and listened to the stories of each race they completed. I wanted what they had, I wanted to tell my story, and I wanted to be an Ironman.

I voiced my interest in doing an Ironman to Fran Campa, one of the Ironman athletes (amateur). For one year we bantered and for some reason I came up with excuses for not doing it. I told myself I did not have enough time, London was a difficult place to train and I suffered knee pain when running. What is more I had my own business to manage. Despite my excuses, Fran kept badgering me to do it. I knew I had a deep desire to complete an Ironman and a conflict raged in my subconscious mind.

I left work in the gym to start a business in South Kensington called Physical Edge Ltd. In the summer of that year I lay down in a park in Ealing and gathered my thoughts together. Would I enter an Ironman or not? I wanted to feel certain I was making the right decision. I had spent hours looking at websites on Ironman races and being inspired by Ironman athletes fighting pain and crossing the finish line.

The certainty I wanted to feel before making my decision to do the Ironman never came to me. I phoned Fran from the park and 'spilled my guts'. I knew I had to make a decision now and the time for thinking was over. I was getting older (35 years old) and my personal time had only got less with each passing year. If I had children my Ironman dream would need to wait again. I challenged Fran over the phone with questions: "Could I do it?" "Will I have the time?" "What is it really like?" My questions were a delaying tactic because I already knew the answers. I took one deep, long breath and made Fran promise he would coach and support me through the training; I could not do it without his help. He committed to making the Ironman happen with me. I breathed out a long, slow sigh and told Fran, "I will do it!" I was going to enter an Ironman and finally make my dream become a reality. I felt fear, excitement and relief all at once.

Fran stepped into his role as head coach with gusto. I had made up my mind but I had not entered an Ironman race yet. He told me to enter the Austria, Germany or Switzerland Ironman because they were ideal for first time Ironman athletes: semi-flat courses, beautiful scenery and professional organisation.

The entry for each Ironman race starts the day after the previous year's race. I watched for the finish of the Austria and Germany races but had trouble entering online. I left it 10 days and regrettably missed the registration deadlines.

The Switzerland Ironman was next and I made sure I registered on time.

I drove to the gym in Fulham and on the public computer I entered the Switzerland Ironman website, paid £450 and registered as an official Ironman competitor. It was August 1st and the race was July 25th the following year. My decision to do an Ironman now felt real and life was about to change.

CHAPTER TWO

Mental game

Entering the Ironman was a big challenge and as much a mental game as it was physical. I decided to empower myself with a set of mental tools before I began to train. These five tools included: Discipline, Powerful Beliefs, Positive Mindset, Law of Attraction and Time Commitment.

Awakening discipline

People say 'crossing a bridge and then burning it' is making a true decision in life. It means moving forward and not being able to turn back once a decision has been made. Once I entered the Ironman, there was no turning back. It was going to be a tough year. If I was going to be successful I had to be disciplined and follow through with my training programme.

In the beginning I relied on my coach to guide me along the way. He was like a safety blanket as I asked him question after question. Once my physical training started, he wanted me to become more independent and find the answers to the questions myself. He wanted me to create my own path to the Ironman and have a unique experience. He gave me general guidance with a specific training programme and left the rest to me. I realised it was my responsibility to complete the Ironman and that discipline would be the key to my success.

I became very disciplined with my training and completed every session in the week. I trained hard and did not complain. Often I wanted to talk to my coach to let him know what I was experiencing. I sounded like I needed a pep talk but I just wanted someone to listen who knew what I was doing. I did everything to the best of my ability and when training got tough I let my fear of the Ironman drive me on. I was afraid I would not train enough to finish the race.

Story

The power of discipline

In the first three months of training I focused on improving my technique for swimming, cycling and running. It took real discipline to begin a routine of training six days a week. I had only been training one day a week doing weights in the gym.

I employed a swimming coach straight away. He showed me what I was doing wrong using video analysis (see www.physical-edge.com YouTube Ironman Series). I was creating drag in the water because my legs were sinking below the line of my body. I was losing forward momentum because my fingers were separated under the water and I was gliding too long with each arm stroke. Watching the video made it easier to see what I was doing wrong. I gradually corrected my technique and reinforced proper movement patterns. I became a stronger swimmer as I repeated these movement patterns from the beginning of Ironman training.

When I started swimming I could only achieve 100 metres before stopping. Some drills were so technical I almost drowned. I remember turning my head to breathe and actually sinking. I could see the surface of the pool getting further away from me as I sank. I eventually mastered these swimming drills over several months; I mastered them because I practised consistently until I got it right. I had the discipline to make every training session count, regardless of how tired I felt or the mayhem going on in the rest of my life. Each time I successfully completed a technical swimming drill it was a mini victory and I celebrated by punching the water triumphantly. It felt good to be successful and I left the pool motivated to improve even more.

Power of belief

The Ironman is a serious race and requires serious commitment. Most people wonder how it is humanly possible to complete the race in one day. I had doubts about the race myself because I had never run a marathon before or combined it with swimming and cycling such long distances.

It was my first Ironman and I was in awe of the challenge ahead. I had a great fear of the actual race because I could not control what was going to happen on the day. I trained for 12 months and the fear was always in my subconscious mind. I ignored it most of the time but when I relaxed and allowed myself to think of the race it returned.

I compare the fear I had to being a passenger on an aeroplane about to land in stormy conditions. My destiny was totally out of my hands. No matter how prepared I was for the Ironman, the outcome on the day was unpredictable. I needed to manage my fear in a positive manner.

I managed my fear successfully by creating a powerful belief about myself. I believed I would finish the Ironman no matter what I had to do. Through this belief I saw the challenges arising in training as opportunities to grow and be better. They were put before me to prepare me physically to complete the Ironman.

I also strengthened this belief with my faith as a Christian. I felt enormous mental pressure leading up to the race. Having God on my side and being able to focus on something greater than the Ironman gave me peace of mind. I was able to hand control of the situation over to God, then relax and enjoy the moment. Once I had done this I was thinking with greater clarity and made better decisions.

Faith works

The two days before the Ironman I had terrible equipment problems with my bike. I was wasting valuable mental and physical energy sorting out the problems. Only my faith in God pulled me through with confidence.

A cardinal rule in triathlon is 'Never change your equipment at the last minute' because untested equipment can fail and result in an early finish to an Ironman's race. I broke this rule and put my race in jeopardy.

I decided to borrow Zipp racing wheels for my bike in the Ironman; I had them for two weeks before the race. I was excited because they increased my flat road racing speed. I bought new tyres to go on the wheels before flying to Zurich in Switzerland. When I got to Zurich the tyres were difficult to put on the wheels because they were too tight. I snapped my tyre levers in half and punctured an inner tube trying to get them on. I realised this would also happen if I got a puncture during the race, and panicked. I went to Ironman Village and asked the bike mechanic to put the tyres on the wheels. He did it with great difficulty and shook his head when he handed them back. His body language suggested I would have a lot of trouble doing it myself.

I went to the afternoon race briefing in Ironman Village where the race officials recommended a specific ratio of gears for bikes to climb the steep mountains in the race. The Zipp wheels I borrowed did not have this gearing so I went back to the bike mechanic and purchased a new rear cassette to correct it.

The bike mechanic put the cassette on my back wheel for three times the normal price. I went for a test ride and heard loud clunking noises as I changed up and down the gears. I took my bike back to the mechanic three times to fine-tune the gear changing. It was still not right so he decided to strip the entire front gear cable off the bike and put a new one on. I retested the bike and the gears still skipped intermittently. I had spent one and a half hours trying to fix the problem and I was tired and stressed. These last-minute changes had put my race in jeopardy.

I could feel myself getting even more tired and stressed as I continued to take my bike backwards and forwards to the bike mechanic to work on it. At this stage of my preparation I should have been resting, eating and conserving energy. I finally decided there was nothing more I could do. I asked God to watch over me and said a prayer, "Lord, please keep my bike from any mechanical failures in the race. Let it run smoothly and get me to the finish line. Thank you for getting me through everything so far. Be with me now in this race, Amen." I placed my bike into transition for the night and did not think about it anymore. After I said the prayer and put the bike into transition I felt the pressure of the situation ease from my mind and I relaxed.

When I look back at the mayhem of that day I realise how my willingness for God to take care of the situation was so beneficial. After the prayer I focused on preparing my physical body for the race and enjoying the moment again. God was alongside me the entire race and I completed the bike course in six and a half hours.

Keeping a positive mindset

Ironman requires a positive mindset because training combined with life is exhausting and it pushes the body to the limit. Injuries can also occur and recovery can be very frustrating.

When I got an injury late in my training, I heard Chrissie Wellington, World Ironman Champion, discuss her strategies for fast recovery. She focused on resting the injured body part and reinforcing her belief that it would heal. She also worked on other areas of her body and race strategy to maximise time and performance. I followed her approach and treated my injuries proactively.

My coaches were also pro-positive thinkers. They kept the environment around me upbeat and fun. I employed a mental conditioning coach to prepare me psychologically for the race. My aim in the race was to absorb the atmosphere, be present and enjoy the experience. I wanted the Ironman to be incredible and having a positive mindset was key to making that possible.

Story

Managing my injury

Two weeks before the Ironman I was racing my bike around Richmond Park. The ground was wet and as I accelerated on a roundabout my back wheel slid from under me and I crashed down on to the road. I felt my hip bleeding and my wrist and shoulder were painful from taking the brunt of the fall.

The next morning I tried to walk but the stiffness and pain in my hip made me limp. My hip had a deep graze over an area the size of a tennis ball. The graze kept bleeding because it stretched each time I flexed my hip. My wrist and shoulder were clicking and any pressure down through my arm created sharp pain in my wrist. I was angry and frustrated because I had been in perfect physical condition leading up to the fall. The thought of pulling out of the Ironman crossed my mind and with two weeks to go to race day I was worried.

I phoned my coach the day after the accident. He knew this was a bad injury but stayed calm and gave me constructive feedback. He wanted me to keep positive at all times. I stopped training for a week and rested; it was hard to stop training but I knew it was the right thing to do.

While I was resting I kept thinking about losing fitness. To combat this negativity I focused instead on healing my injuries as quickly as possible. I discovered wet dressings for my hip wound which kept the environment around the graze clean and moist to aid in faster healing. I changed the dressings daily and applied healing gel underneath. I treated my own shoulder and wrist with physiotherapy. Watching my injuries get better each day made me feel happier.

After a week of rest, my coach wanted me to run for one hour to test the pain in my hip. Twenty minutes into the run I felt severe knee pains and stopped immediately. My leg muscles had stiffened from the bike accident and inactivity during my week of rest. Old ITB (Iliotibial Band) problems around my knees had returned. I asked myself fearfully, "How am I going to run a marathon in seven days?" I phoned my coach with the news. He gave me strict instructions to stop all training. My next run would be the marathon in the Ironman. I thought to myself, 'What sort of advice is that?' But that is exactly what I had to do.

I flew to Switzerland and for two days before the race I massaged my legs constantly. I spent one and a half hours massaging every evening. I did not know what would happen when I started running the marathon but I knew a positive mindset was important. I spent time preparing my transition bag and race nutrition. I liked talking to other people around me to keep my mind busy. Having my coach with me in Switzerland and laughing really helped my mood. We bantered all the time and banned any talk of injuries.

Standing on the start line for the Ironman I knew I had done everything possible to heal my injuries. My leg muscles felt flexible and the wound had healed. I entered Lake Zurich to start the swim and trusted everything would be OK.

Law of Attraction

Training for an Ironman is a personal journey and no two athletes will train the same. There are many ways to train, and as a first timer with no experience it was overwhelming to think about it.

There is a law called the Law of Attraction; I had learnt this in a personal development course. When you set your mind on something and you really want it, you will attract what you need to yourself. For it to work, you must see and live what you want in your imagination. If you believe it is real, it is projected into your life and becomes a reality.

I used the Law of Attraction right from the start of my training. I imagined everything falling into place, keeping an open mind and taking action to get things done. I wanted to start training fast and it was exciting to think what I was about to do.

Story

Power of attraction

Each week I learned more about being an Ironman. I bought the correct equipment for swimming, biking and running so I could train through the bitterly cold English winter. Slowly and steadily my knowledge grew and I met people who were to help with my training.

I went to a physiotherapy conference and met an elite level nutritionist. When he heard I was doing the Ironman he offered to help with my eating plan. A bike mechanic at my local triathlon store offered to do my bike fit. I met a mental conditioning coach through a mutual friend and he offered a visualisation recording for my entire race. Things were attracted into my life the more I wanted help. I was always thinking ahead on what needed to be done next and when something I wanted presented itself I knew when to grab it.

The Ironman required careful planning throughout the year because I was also managing my own business and had organised trips away for weddings, holidays and physiotherapy courses. Some of these trips were during the most intense and important months of training. I trusted in the Law of Attraction and that everything would work out.

Of the six most important weeks of training I could only complete two of them. My coach decided to drop my training sessions to three a week instead of six. I only trained the longest distances for each discipline each week. When I travelled away I rested and the plan worked brilliantly. During this period, some days were very long but I managed my time wisely. Some mornings I did not want to get out of bed. It was my fear of the Ironman and enjoyment for training motivating me to get up at these times.

I completed all my training targets for the Ironman and I know the Law of Attraction helped. My clear vision of finishing the Ironman attracted the things I needed to me. It worked because I was 100% committed to Ironman and passionate about training.

Time commitment

The time it takes to train for an Ironman will vary depending on the training programme set by your coach each week. The advantages of training for one year are changing the training plan if needed and having time to recover from injuries. The thought of training for an Ironman sounds ominous; however it is less demanding than you think.

Story

The facts

I trained for my Ironman over one year. Training was broken down into smaller chunks consisting of one long and one short distance session each week for each discipline. In the first 10.5 months I built my training distances up to a 45-minute swim, a three-hour bike ride and a one and a half hour run.

My longest training sessions started after ten and a half months and lasted two weeks. The longest distances for each discipline included a one and a quarter hour swim, a six-hour bike ride and a two and a half hour run. After two weeks I tapered (reduced my training) to race day to allow my body to rest and prepare for the full Ironman distances.

The challenge when starting Ironman training is to fit six days in a week. I achieved this by routinely blocking out time in my diary each week. I found the short training sessions were very manageable. My long sessions were completed after work or on weekends.

When I compared training for the Ironman to training for the Etape du Tour (cycle stage of the Tour de France), I found the Etape du Tour more challenging on my time because my cycle sessions ranged from two to eight hours, four to five times per week.

Training for the Ironman is manageable if you can be organised. I use the word manageable because I did rush between work, social activities and training to keep life together. I had challenges finding time to eat and sleep properly and without doubt I experienced extreme fatigue. This is all part of the Ironman experience and I pushed myself to keep going.

An Ironman will change your time priorities. It cannot be taken lightly and if you are time-short because of business, relationships, children and travel then you will need to be even tighter with your organisational skills. Personally, the bigger the sacrifice I made in my life to train, the more it meant to finish the Ironman. Just look at my finishing photo and you can see what it meant to me (www.physical-edge.com).

To keep my personal relationship alive during Ironman training I communicated clearly with my girlfriend what was going to happen. I made sure she knew my training schedule and when I would spend quality time with her. She understood how tired I felt at the end of the day and kept socially busy with girlfriends. She liked to know there was an end date to all the madness and looked forward to seeing me finish the race. I thanked her for being very patient with me during training but I also knew she loved telling her friends she was dating an Ironman.

Completing an Ironman is character-changing. I developed and strengthened several powerful character traits during training. These included an extreme ability to focus and achieve an outcome, incredible discipline, stamina under physical pain and mental stress and supreme organisational skills. It sounds tough but the journey is amazing and full of emotion. It could be a once in a lifetime achievement and it is made all the sweeter by the challenges it presents.

TIPS

1. *Make the decision to do an Ironman by paying the money and entering*
2. *Always be disciplined to complete your training goals*
3. *Create powerful beliefs to pull you through the tough times*

Most of all, have fun and enjoy the journey

CHAPTER THREE

Coaches make it less effort and do it the right way

When I decided to do the Ironman I wanted to have a team working with me like a professional athlete. The team approach was a rewarding experience and each specialist played an important role in my success. The team included a head coach, swim coach, bike mechanic, nutritionist, massage therapist and mental conditioning coach. I was the physiotherapist in the team.

Head coach

Having a great coach who has done an Ironman before is the key to a successful race. A coach takes away the uncertainty of knowing what to do and provides advice on all areas of training. Without my coach I could not have completed the Ironman with such confidence and trained like a professional.

My coach was also a personal trainer and worked from a gym. He had wanted to learn how to swim and decided an Ironman would motivate him to achieve it. He has now completed seven Ironman races and continues to compete around the world. He is a strong runner and a fast hill-climber on the bike. In the past he was in the military and trained as a sniper; he then completed his law degree before moving on to Ironman coaching. I valued my coach because he was excellent at assessing any situation objectively and giving common sense advice.

I chose my coach (amateur athlete) over a coach who was a professional Ironman athlete because he understood what it was like to work and train. He also lived in the same area I did and knew where to access resources locally.

The first thing my coach taught me was what not to do. I had no experience of Ironman training so really did not know what I was doing. At first I bought the 220 triathlon magazine and read reviews about equipment. I wanted to buy £1,500 wheels and a bike worth £7,000 even though I had a bike already.

My coach sat me down and said I did not need to spend money on a new bike. He explained, "It is the machine on the bike that makes the difference and not the bike." In other words, training my body was more important than buying an expensive bike. I was disappointed but understood that spending £8,500 on bike and wheels would not give me the speed I imagined it would.

I also wanted to train with a triathlon club, but he warned me not to because in a group situation I had to train at the pace set by the fastest person. This would upset my own rhythm and training needs.

My coach's early advice saved me time, money and got me focused on what was most important: technique and training.

Story

How training worked

My coach gave me a week's training programme every Sunday. Before he gave me the programme we spoke on the phone and I gave him feedback on how my body felt, what problems I had combining training with work and what social commitments I had planned. Each week the training programme was altered to fit with my specific circumstances.

Getting a training programme each week was very different from my previous coaching experience. In the past I was given the entire programme at the start of training. I was used to knowing what was going to happen ahead of time and could prepare for it.

At first I was annoyed at receiving my training programme at the beginning of each week. However, after a few months I started to enjoy regular contact with my coach.

I valued highly the opportunity to tell him how I was going in training and change my programme to suit what was happening in my life. He knew exactly what I was going through and was always asking for regular updates on my progress. I blindly trusted him and at times felt like a soldier following the commands of his captain. This approach was necessary to get the results I wanted and set me up perfectly for the Ironman race.

Swim coach

Even though I had a coach, I felt I needed a team of people to support me through the Ironman. My experience as a physiotherapist for elite athletes highlighted the value of having several coaches for each area of the sport. My goal was to be the best I could be and have an unforgettable experience and therefore I wanted help with my swimming.

My swimming was my greatest fear in the triathlon and getting my technique correct was a priority early on in my training. The swim leg in the triathlon is not the longest of the three disciplines but it can be the most challenging and a scary proposition if you do not swim much.

When an Ironman race starts, over 2,000 swimmers are fighting for space in the water. If the space of water is small then you are hit by thrashing legs and arms all around you. Swimmers push you left and right and are in front and behind you; they can even swim over the top of you if you let them. In my race I was kicked in the stomach, grabbed by the legs and pulled back. I was also elbowed in the face and pushed aside around the markers. Having good swimming technique and speed enabled me to accelerate away from some of these dangerous situations. It saved me valuable energy for the remainder of the race.

My first swim session

My coach contacted a swimming specialist and we met early on a Saturday morning to assess where I was currently with my swimming technique. I arrived in large swimming trunks as I did not have my triathlon swimming shorts yet. I was analysed with an underwater video camera. I could see clearly how I was creating drag. Drag is resistance to forward movement in the water and reduces swimming speed and efficiency. The longest distance I could swim continuously that day was 50 metres. I was freaking out as I needed to swim 3.8 kilometres.

We watched the video on a big television screen together (see www.physical-edge.com YouTube video on Ironman Series). My legs were kicking out to the side and hanging low in the water. My arms were moving out of time and my fingers were splayed instead of held together. My trunk was not rotating well, making my shoulders work. All these problems meant I expended excessive energy trying to overcome the drag, and at 50 metres I was exhausted and gasping for air.

Over six sessions the swimming specialist modified my technique. He called me a 'Barracuda' so I could visualise being fast, side-on like a fish and able to cut through the water. Swimming was the most technical of the three sports but as I got better I could swim further and further with less effort. The swimming drills I practised by myself made all the difference.

I was also given advice on how to transition quickly out of my wetsuit and what checks I should do before the swim starts. I was taught to assess any undercurrents in the water, how to find my bike coming out of the swim and what direction I had to run to leave transition. All these tips raised my confidence on race day.

Bike mechanic

While I was learning to swim, my coach instructed me to get a bike fit because I was very uncomfortable in profile position. My neck and hands were painful from the body position my bike forced me to adopt. Now was the time to sort out this problem.

Story

Bike mechanic

My coach introduced me to a bike mechanic in my local triathlon store. I was assessed riding my bike on a turbo trainer (device to allow stationary cycling) in the upright and profile (aerobar) positions. I had previously been fitted to my bike at Cyclefit (a specialist cycle shop) but was still very uncomfortable. I was stretched too far forward which over-extended my neck and put too much pressure through my hands. Over 45 minutes the mechanic tweaked the position of my handlebars and seat. I immediately felt better and over the next three to six months further adjustments were made to improve my comfort on the bike even more. I was also advised to buy a new gel seat and without doubt this was a painless decision.

I highly recommend using a bike mechanic you trust and who races bikes. He saved me hours of pain in training and ensured my bike worked smoothly over the winter and summer months. He even came to my house to fix emergency breakdowns as I got closer to race day.

Nutritionist

The next professional I met was at a physiotherapy conference and he was a nutritionist. He had done Ironman races before and volunteered to help me prepare for mine. My coach and I had dinner with him and discussed my nutritional regime. He said every athlete has to find what works best for his/her body. The principles were: drink three to four litres of water per day, eat small meals six times per day and eat good quality carbohydrates and protein. I would also need recovery drinks, gels and carbohydrate bars. He advised me to try different brands of energy products until I found the brands I liked and then stick to them.

When I was training six days a week I was hungry every two to four hours. Sometimes I ate what was available to me because at work I was very short of time. I remember eating at Subway, Pret A Manger and Carluccio's because they were the closest eateries to me. I do not recommend eating regularly at these places as the food is high in fat and poor quality carbohydrates. When I did eat properly I noticed a significant difference in my energy levels and I was able to recover quicker than normal.

The key to eating well is to learn the amount and type of food to optimise your body's performance. It is an experiment, and with good basic knowledge from a nutritionist you can find what works best for you.

Sports massage

I started training six days a week and my muscles became extremely tight. My calf and quadriceps muscles were the most affected. It did not help when I trained in the gym pushing heavy squats and lunges and then running the following day. The lack of a rest day increased the tightness in my legs even more. After three months I decided to get a sports massage once a week.

In the first session the therapist assessed where on my body I needed treatment. She kept clinical notes of what was important and how I responded to each session. The massages helped to heal my injuries faster; I came out of each massage session feeling more flexible.

I liked my sports massage therapist because she knew the level of pressure to exert on my muscles without creating unbearable pain. She took an interest in my training and was very positive and supportive. The massage session was the only time I lay down to rest during the day and in the session I could switch off mentally from my life and training. I really looked forward to my hour of massage each week.

Mental conditioning coach

The final member of my team was a mental conditioning coach; I met him through a mutual friend. He specialised in preparing Ironman athletes mentally for race day. I had seen the benefits of being trained psychologically for peak performance. He offered to help me six weeks before the Ironman race. His work above all else had the greatest impact on my emotional enjoyment of the Ironman.

We chatted in our first session over Skype and got clarity on what my outcomes for race day would be. My focus was enjoying the experience, having fun and absorbing the entire atmosphere. I did not want to be overly intense or serious about the race because I was not trying to win. I wanted to make sure I finished the race and enjoyed my friends who were supporting me.

In the next two sessions he got to know me very well; he led each session with his in-depth knowledge of my fears, aspirations and blockages. We decided to create a one-hour audio of my perfect race day. It started with me standing on the beach waiting for the bell to ring to start the Ironman. Everything I wanted to hear, see and feel during the entire race was embedded into the audio. He used my own words to motivate me when times got tough. It was like hypnosis and the first time we did the audio session I finished feeling excited, ready to race and on a high. I listened to this audio every night and in the morning for the three days leading up to and including race day.

One of the best visualisations from the audio was running towards the finish line and crossing it. I saw myself celebrating and punching the air triumphantly (see finishing photo). When I crossed the finish line I hugged and thanked my friends for being with me the entire race and cheering me along. I had a huge smile on my face and was in a state of euphoria.

Benefits

Working with each member of my support team was the best decision I made in Ironman training. Their years of experience and bespoke advice proved invaluable. They accelerated my learning and I could see the benefits of their work in my results. They were all passionate about Ironman and their enthusiasm rubbed off on me. They supported me from the start of my training right through to the finish of my race.

I appreciated their expertise and also their friendship and completing the Ironman with their support made the experience a richer one. They were positive, motivational and more than once went beyond what was expected of them to deliver. I now believe an Ironman must have this type of support team to ensure a successful race and to make it an incredible experience.

Story

Half Ironman to Ironman

I completed the Half Ironman six weeks before the Ironman; I now had six weeks to double all my distances in training. I wondered if I had trained enough but my coach said I was on track with his programme. It was an unusual situation as my body was telling me I was not ready but my coach was telling me I was doing fine. I trusted my coach as he had completed six Ironman races by this stage and knew what my body could achieve.

My training increased sharply over the next four weeks. At four weeks I was able to swim four kilometres, ride 160 kilometres and run two and a half hours, all individually. I did not combine any of these long distances until the Ironman. I tapered with two weeks to go to race day. My distances in training reduced but the intensity of my training increased. One week before Ironman I was feeling healthy, fit and strong. I was in the best shape of my life thanks to my Ironman support team.

TIPS

1. *You will need a coach to do Ironman*
2. *A team provides emotional as well as technical support*
3. *Build strong relationships with your team and they go the extra mile*

CHAPTER FOUR

You can train anywhere

When I committed to the Ironman an important question came to mind: 'How was I going to train in London?' The footpaths were uneven, it gets dark at 4.30 p.m. in the winter and there are no lights on country roads. It was a challenge at first but with the help of my coaches and research I managed to find regular places to train. These places were close to where I lived and chosen to make training easier.

Swim training location

My first challenge was to find a swimming pool at least 33 metres long which allowed me to use my wetsuit. I began swimming in an LA Fitness gym. It was a two-minute walk from work. The pool was only 17.5 metres long but it was perfect for technique training at the start. When I increased my swimming distances the pool was too short for developing a good rhythm and endurance.

I searched the internet for the longest pools in London and found the Leisure Centre in Putney with a 33 metre pool. I started swimming in the mornings and enjoyed the extra distance I could swim with each length. Having fewer lengths to count was also a psychological advantage when swimming two to four kilometres. I found swimming between 6.00 a.m. and 9.00 a.m. the quietest time in the pool. Overtaking breaststrokers was good practice for accelerating in short bursts.

Towards the end of winter my swimming coach mentioned a 90 metre pool in Tooting Bec called the Lido. I did not believe him until I saw it with my own eyes. It was an open air pool and allowed the use of wetsuits. In early spring I took my wetsuit to the Lido and jumped in. It was so cold my hands and feet felt like they were in a fridge-freezer.

I swam one length of the pool and it felt endless. I had to look ahead to make sure I was swimming in a straight line. I soon navigated by picking a landmark at each end of the pool and swimming towards it; this was good practice for swimming in open water where sighting the buoy is important. I appreciated my ability to breathe on both sides of my body because I could see each side of the pool and other swimmers beside me.

My first swim in the Lido was one and a half kilometres. I had a wetsuit on but I was very cold at the end. My trunk was cold and my core temperature was dropping. I got out and changed quickly. Swimming in the Lido in summer was a much warmer and enjoyable experience.

Cycle training location

The longest training sessions were my bike rides. They started at 45 minutes and gradually increased to six hours. I lived close to Richmond Park, a common place to ride, and my coach had me training there for six months. The park had a 10 kilometre loop inside it with a combination of long and short hill climbs. It was good for speed training and long distance training. I rode once during the week and once on Sunday.

At the end of six months I was riding for three hours or completing nine laps of Richmond Park. I was by myself most of the time and now I wanted a change of scenery. My coach decided it was time to take me to Windsor. The London to Windsor looped ride took three hours; it was through country roads and a welcome change. The first time I rode to Windsor was with my coach; he led the way and I followed blindly. I was not paying attention to the bike course and when I rode by myself the second time I got lost. In fact I got lost the third time as well. Each time I got lost I trusted my instincts to get me home and made it. It is important to experiment with bike courses in training. The Windsor course became my regular Sunday ride.

My favourite time to ride was in the morning when no one else was around. Richmond Park had a light mist covering its fields. The sun was rising and the wild deer were walking leisurely through the long grass. I could ride my bike silently around the inner road and enjoy the scenery.

Cycle training with a turbo trainer indoors

Sometimes riding my bike outside in winter was dangerous because the roads were icy and it was dark. At these times I trained on a turbo trainer. This is a stationary platform to which I attach the back wheel of my bike and it lifts it off the ground. It allows me to ride like a stationary bike in the gym. It has a separate lever to increase and decrease resistance.

Story

Long night

One night the weather was terrible so I decided to train on my turbo trainer for two and a half hours. My coach never told me about chaffing cream to stop friction of my groin on the bike seat. It was the most painful training session I ever did because the turbo trainer locked the bike in one place and increased friction on my groin even more.

For two and a half hours I was incredibly uncomfortable on the turbo trainer. I managed to get temporary relief by standing up on the pedals, off the bike seat, to let blood flow back to my vital areas. After the turbo trainer session I had pain in my groin for two days. I was glad I only did four turbo trainer sessions over the entire winter.

Run training location

My running was my weakest discipline in the Ironman. I had run a half marathon in two hours before and I expected the marathon to take me five hours. In the past I had suffered from ITB Friction Syndrome in both my knees. When I ran for more than 20 minutes the band down the outside of each knee rubbed over a bone and created pain. The pain increased and then the knees would lock. The worse surfaces to run on were cambered roads and down hills.

My coach had me run on a treadmill for 30 minutes to one hour for the first three months of training. Treadmill running did not irritate my knees as it was flat and offered more shock absorption compared to the roads.

I also started Pilates to strengthen my trunk and leg muscles to prevent ITB Friction Syndrome. I practised moving my legs with correct alignment to reinforce good biomechanics. I went once a week and exercised on the Cadillac, Reformer and mats. In between my weekly sessions I did home exercise drills on the floor. After 10 weeks I started to run outside.

I was very careful choosing the surfaces I ran on outside. I started running from work in South Kensington to Battersea Park. In Battersea Park was a four kilometre inner ring road. It took me 22 minutes to complete one lap and I knew if I got knee pain it was a short walk back to South Kensington.

After running round Battersea Park a few times I noticed pain in both my knees. The road was designed to drain water and it had a slope going down the right and left side of the centre line. I tried running on the centre line to keep the pressure off my knees but the camber eventually irritated them.

To increase my running distance I needed roads with no camber. I decided to run around Putney where I lived. The footpaths were less cambered and my knees could tolerate them. Each time I went for a run I searched for long flat roads and eventually found a comfortable running route to train on.

In my two to three hour training sessions I ran from Putney to Ealing. The route had shops for me to buy water and toilets to use. I remember seeing friends having lunch along the way. The longest run I did was two and a half hours. I interspersed speed sessions with long runs to help me get quicker. Once I was comfortable with my running route I never changed it.

TIPS

1. *Find locations convenient to home and work*

2. *The training terrain must be suitable for any injuries*

3. *Winter training may be indoors sometimes*

CHAPTER FIVE

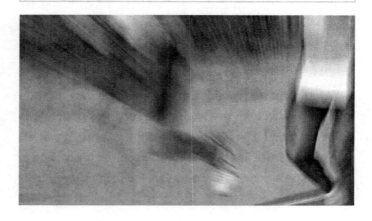

Structure of training

Training for an Ironman involves three disciplines. The basic structure of training is to train each discipline twice a week; this would include one short session and one long session. The reason why you do not have to train more for each discipline is the crossover effect of training between them; for example, when you train your legs in cycling you develop strength to run.

Swim sessions

Short swim sessions involved drills from my swimming coach for 45 minutes to one hour. These drills had me swimming on my side and with variations of arm movements to mimic swimming like a fish. Strengthening my kicking helped raise my legs in the water.

These drills also improved my trunk rotation and synchronisation of my arm strokes to make me a more efficient swimmer. I had less drag in the water and I increased my speed. In six months I was able to swim comfortably for one kilometre.

Once I had good swimming technique my long swim sessions increased dramatically. I remember my coach telling me to swim one and a half kilometres and then four kilometres in a very short time frame. Long sessions were designed to get my body accustomed to swimming for distance. Speed was less of an importance. I liked to finish my swim sessions strongly so I always started slowly and got faster the further I swam.

Story

The secret is to draft

My swim in the Ironman was tough because water visibility was poor and swimmers were pushing each other for space around the markers on the course. I could feel the energy it took for me to accelerate away from other swimmers or fight them off.

I could not see the markers on the course when I was swimming and I knew I had to conserve as much energy as possible for the rest of the race. When I found a swimmer who was about my speed and heading in the right direction I decided to draft him. Drafting means following right behind him to reduce water resistance against me. When I drafted a swimmer I was faster and I could relax into a good rhythm. I highly recommend drafting in the swim leg of the Ironman because it is 3.8 kilometres long.

Bike sessions

The hills around Richmond Park were useful for short bike sessions. My coach set me 'hill repeats' to complete. This involved a 150-metre sprint to the base of a 50-metre hill and then a climb to the top as fast as possible. I would turn around at the top, coast to the bottom and then repeat the climb again. I had 10 repeats to do in one session. My heart rate reached 90% of maximum in the climbs. These sessions shattered me but I could feel my legs get stronger as well.

When I first completed the hill repeats I felt faint at the top of the hill. I realised my rib cage was stiff and restricted my breathing; it reduced oxygen to my brain and I felt faint. My body needed releasing and I went to my massage therapist and a physiotherapist for help.

The physiotherapist released myofascial structures around my chest and rib cage and the massage therapist worked on surrounding areas. I also took a magnesium and calcium supplement to replace minerals lost from sweating.

After the treatment and supplementation my maximum heart rate increased and I was able to climb faster up the hills. I also noticed I was more comfortable on my bike on long rides.

I completed my long rides on weekends. I usually went alone but occasionally my coach came out with me and we rode to Windsor and back again. I used these long rides to practise riding at race pace. This meant riding at the speed I would ride 180 kilometres in the Ironman.

I learned to listen to my body as I tested it on longer and longer rides. I could choose the right gears for hill climbing and riding on flat roads. I focused on eating regularly to sustain good energy levels at all times. I enjoyed the long bike sessions because they were more like the race and I felt a sense of achievement when I finished.

Run training

My short run sessions were set at a speed faster than race pace. My legs felt strong from cross training, i.e. swimming and cycling. I often used landmarks as targets to motivate me to run faster; the Fulham football ground and Putney Bridge were significant landmarks.

I wore my full triathlon kit when I ran to get used to it. I looked like a professional athlete and running home as fast as possible was not my real race pace but looked impressive. I usually kept my short run sessions to one hour. These sessions were for toughness like the short sessions for swimming and cycling.

Long run sessions were about maintaining good technique. It still amazes me that the longest I ran in training was two and a half hours and in the Ironman I ran for five hours. These runs were long enough to require eating and drinking; I took power bars and bought water in shops I ran past. When I finished these runs it was a great success as I never found running easy. I was particularly pleased when my body felt good.

In triathlon there is a great variety of training to do. The variety kept me mentally stimulated and physically challenged for an entire year. I was constantly learning and experimenting with the effects of training on my body. There were targets to hit and then new ones to set. The urgency to achieve distances or learn new skills in training kept the excitement alive.

Story

Mistake in racing

I completed a Half Ironman in Cornwall as part of my training for the Ironman. The week before the race I rode around Richmond Park too fast. I damaged my thigh muscles and they never recovered fully before the race. They felt extremely tight and tired, especially walking downstairs.

The bike leg in the Half Ironman was a hilly course. I thought the hills were 10 kilometres long but they continued for 80 kilometres instead. My left thigh muscle started to cramp and in the last five kilometres it locked my leg straight as I accelerated up a hill. I almost fell off my bike. The muscle cramped again and again when I pushed my legs too hard so I rode slowly back to transition to start the run leg.

It was not surprising to find the run leg of the triathlon was also a hilly course. One hill climbed as far as my eyes could see. It was so long the runners at the top of the hill looked like ants in the distance. I put my head down, looked at the ground ahead and focused on one step at a time.

The run had two laps and in the second lap my hamstrings and thigh muscles were cramping painfully. I never stopped running but I did slow down. This slow run is called the 'Ironman Shuffle' in triathlon. It does not look pretty but it did get me home.

TIPS

1. *Get a structured training programme from a coach*
2. *Get clarity on what you need to do for each training session*
3. *Be disciplined and follow instructions*

CHAPTER SIX

Training finesse

Training for an Ironman starts with gym sessions to build a good base of strength, endurance and power. Technique sessions are also included for each of the three disciplines: swim, bike and run. This was my focus for the first five months of training and it gave me time for quality learning and practice.

The gym training for my legs included squats, single leg lunges and dead lifts. I only trained bench press and triceps extensions for my upper body to help with swimming. When my squats had increased to 120kg the pressure on my knees became too much. At this point my coach changed me to strength training drills when swimming, biking and running. It was nice to get out of the gym and into the outdoors more often. The change of training was earlier than expected but, as with all my training, it was adapted if my body felt pain.

Story

How I felt stronger on my bike

When I started bike training in Richmond Park I noticed how slow I was on the hills. Other riders appeared to glide past me effortlessly. When I tried to ride faster my legs filled with lactic acid and my heart could not maintain the pace. Eventually I discovered the speed and cadence at which I was comfortable riding. I called this my race pace as I was able to maintain it without fatiguing; it was 30km/hr and 90 RPM (revolutions per minute).

After six months of training, through hellish winter weather, I noticed my strength on the bike had improved dramatically. Riding up the hills in Richmond Park no longer hurt as much. There were riders struggling up the hills as I had been at the start but now I was accelerating past them. My breathing got easier and my recovery rate got faster. I enjoyed riding past other riders because it was a sign to me of better fitness. It also felt good going faster than someone else.

I practised riding in aero position and keeping a steady pace around the entire park. Three laps of the park seemed a long way at the start but I soon increased to eight or nine laps. By this point I was riding for three to four hours. It was mind-numbing work but it created a strong base fitness for the second half of the year.

Technique

The technique sessions were more mental exercises than physical. They helped change the way I moved to make me more efficient and effective over longer distances in the swim, bike and run.

Swim technique

It took me six lessons over seven months to train my body to swim differently. I would have a lesson, practise by myself, and when I was ready to progress arrange the next lesson. The rate of my improvement depended on the quality of my practice.

Story

Swim technique and swimming faster

The best swim I had was a two kilometre swim in my local pool. I got permission from the manager to wear my wetsuit. It took me 800 metres to get into my rhythm but after that I swam strongly. When other swimmers stopped to rest I kept going; I was a swimming machine.

I swam 60 lengths of the pool that day and in the last 100 metres I sprinted. This swim gave me a lot of confidence.

Other swimmers also noticed me swim that day. After finishing, a swimmer in an adjacent lane asked me how I managed to swim so long and keep such a steady speed. As I explained my training to him it occurred to me how far I had come. When I started I could swim 50 metres and now it was two kilometres.

Cycle technique

I was fortunate to have a great coach who taught me how to ride my bike correctly for Ironman. I could not watch myself ride so he offered to ride with me and give me feedback.

We met at Richmond Park at 9.00 a.m. and planned a three and a half hour ride to Windsor and back again. Before we started my coach stressed the importance of safety at all times. I was to practise good steering control and follow closely behind his back wheel. He had hand signals for overtake, slow down and take the lead.

We rode out of the suburban streets and into the countryside where there was less traffic. My coach relaxed into his race pace. I rode behind him and carefully watched his gear changing, how he handled the bike on flats and hills and when he ate and drank. I noted the speed he was riding and the cadence he used. As I was watching him I remembered I had a marathon to run in the Ironman after the bike leg. I thought if I exerted my legs too hard on the bike I would 'Bonk' (Bonk means run out of carbohydrate stored in my leg muscles) and probably not finish the marathon and the Ironman. I practised riding at a steady race pace.

I shadowed every gear change my coach made, everything he ate and drank and any change in his riding position. I learned more from this ride than any other in my training. We stopped in Windsor and discussed what I was doing. I got feedback for the return ride to Richmond Park and practised what I had learned.

I continued to practise my riding technique over the next nine months of training and the ride to Windsor and back got faster. My coach did accompany me on a few more rides, which further developed my biking skills. He thought my cycling was my strongest discipline.

Story

Putting me in my place

I thought I was riding much better after nine months and wanted to beat my coach. The test I used was a short steep hill in Richmond Park called Spankers Hill. As we approached it my coach took the lead. I was determined to stay with him to the top and followed him closely.

The gradient of the hill increased sharply and my coach changed into a harder gear; I did the same. He suddenly accelerated. I tried to follow but my legs started to burn. No matter how hard I told my legs to push they wouldn't go any faster. He accelerated away from me and finished 20 metres ahead.

My coach had been riding for five years and developed enormous strength in his legs for hill climbing. I thought I could match him but I realised he was a much better rider. He had emphatically reminded me he was the coach and I was the 'grasshopper' or disciple.

Running technique

My coach analysed my running technique on a treadmill. From his analysis he advised me to relax my shoulders and swing my arms just in front of my body, let my trunk muscles and arms propel me forward. Making these changes reduced the amount of work my legs had to do.

My new running technique worked well for me. I was able to maintain the same technique and speed from the start to the end of my long runs. I could use my trunk and arms to increase my running speed. Running was my slowest discipline in Ironman and these subtle changes kept my pace steady throughout the marathon.

Story

Blowing my legs out running

The first time my coach asked me to run faster than race pace for one and a half hours I thought he meant run as fast as I could for one and a half hours. He actually meant run just above the pace for a marathon.

I sprinted out of the door of my clinic in South Kensington like a rampaging buffalo, swerving past pedestrians in my way and jumping curbs. I ran in the direction of Regents Park and circled it twice.

After sprinting for 30 minutes I could feel my legs begin to tighten. Both my knees hurt and I was quickly running out of energy. I thought my coach was mad making me run this fast for so long. Giving up was on my mind but I was determined to continue. I slowed down because it was impossible to maintain the pace. My sprint became a jog.

I was sweating profusely and getting really hungry. In my backpack I carried three carbohydrate shots so I drank them all quickly. This helped my energy levels but the pain in my knees got slowly worse. Over the next 30 minutes I wanted to stop several times but I knew each training session was important and pushed myself to continue.

It felt good to be heading home after an hour of running. My legs were more painful than ever and my jog had almost become a fast walk. When I reached South Kensington I was physically and mentally shattered. I lay on the floor motionless and slowly recovered.

I called my coach to tell him about my run. We both did not understand why I suffered so much. I thought I was under training and not fit enough. When we realised I had been running too fast it was no surprise I was so sore. It was important I made this mistake before the Ironman and not during the Ironman. It took me a week to recover and I controlled my running speed much better from that day onwards.

Recovery

Recovery helps the body respond to training and is used to good effect by professional athletes. After a strong stimulus (training session) and then rest, the body adapts by getting even stronger. If the balance between training and rest is poor, athletes can suffer overtraining syndrome. Overtraining can lead to injury and substandard performance.

Story

Overtraining

I pushed myself to the limit. I trained hard and worked hard and had late nights. I woke up in the morning feeling sick from tiredness with a long working day ahead. At work my concentration wavered and I occasionally had to sleep.

It was a tough balance jumping between training, work and maintaining relationships with friends, family and a girlfriend. In my year of training I did not get enough sleep. On rest days I kept doing things when I really needed to stay at home and sleep.

I know tiredness is part of Ironman training but it can be managed. My problem was I chose not to rest when I had the opportunity. I think I pushed myself too hard and over-trained at times. In hindsight I would recommend to other Ironman athletes to get rest as the therapeutic and performance benefits are massive.

TIPS

1. *Build a base of muscular strength early in training*
2. *Focus on correct technique before long distance training*
3. *Optimise recovery for greatest results*

CHAPTER SEVEN

Train the way you play

My coach believed you 'train the way you play'. In other words, when you train, replicate what you do in the real race. This includes your focus, clothing, eating, transitions etc. The more you practise what you do in the real race, the more familiar you become with it. If you have trained successfully before, over and over again, then your chances of a successful race are higher.

Story

Stern reminder

Sometimes I could be training on my bike for three to six hours and running for one to three hours. This was a long time to be listening to myself think so I used an iPod to play my favourite dance music and keep myself motivated. As I listened to the music my mind relaxed and I escaped the monotony of training.

I was seven months into my training and my coach heard me say I was using an iPod. He ordered me to stop immediately. The thought of training without my music seemed ridiculous. He explained that iPods are dangerous as you cannot hear the traffic around you, also on race day you will not have an iPod, so practise without it. The race is 13-14 hours long and it is a solitary experience. In his words, "Get used to it."

He told me to focus on how my body was feeling during the training, learn to listen to the bike and my surroundings. Get more accustomed to quiet times and being alone. This replicated the Ironman race.

In the end I stopped training with my iPod. It helped me connect more with the experience of racing. The awareness of my body, equipment and surroundings magnified tenfold. I was able to detect and alter my training if my body did not feel right and I knew if something was wrong with my bike. Some days I stopped training because the conditions were too dangerous.

Having better awareness of my body, equipment and surroundings did make a difference on race day. I had over 2,000 other athletes around me in an unfamiliar country. I felt confident I was able to make the adjustments in my race depending on how I felt and what was happening around me.

I remember in the swim leg I knew I was starting to tire in the final straight home so adjusted my pace to get me to the end. In the bike leg I had gear-changing problems. I was aware when the chain was going to slip or come off and rode slower to avoid it. In the run leg I felt my body was hungrier than normal so I stopped to eat more at aid stations. I finished the marathon without 'hitting the wall'. All these adjustments were important in my successful Ironman race.

Flexibility

Training for an Ironman requires discipline and the training programme was carefully structured to get the results I wanted. If I missed a training session I knew there would be consequences to my race performance at a later date.

Despite my determination to follow the programme to the word, I often changed it because my work and social engagements were also important. Training did come first but there were times when it was not realistic to compromise my work or social commitments.

Being flexible at the right time saved me unnecessary stress and probably injuries. It also helped me cope with difficult situations before the Ironman.

Ironman in Zurich

I travelled to Zurich to race the Ironman. I had never been to this city before and I had two days to prepare for my race. The simplest tasks such as finding restaurants, supermarkets and pharmacies now required internet searches and maps. I had a plan for my ideal race preparation but unexpected things happened and it had to change.

I wanted to do a swim in Lake Zurich the day before the race. When I got to the lake edge it had been roped off for a shorter distance triathlon race. I did not get to swim. It rained heavily for two days before the Ironman so I lost the opportunity to test my bike equipment and bike train. The race village was a long walk from the city centre and I wasted valuable energy reserves getting there and back.

The only reason I stayed calm and got everything done was that I remained flexible and adapted to each situation individually. I had practised being flexible in my training all year and it now helped to be flexible in Zurich. The importance of each situation was greater in Zurich but I successfully made the best decisions on the day and still enjoyed myself. I remembered my goal of enjoying the journey I was on as it was a once in a lifetime experience. Being flexible is a great test for any Ironman.

Training abroad

Ironman training is relentless. No matter what is happening in your life it is a necessity to train. This could mean training when travelling overseas. I had to do this in New Zealand (NZ) and it was a compete reverse in my training conditions.

Story

Upside down

I planned my training in NZ months in advance. I booked my bike on to the plane and arranged my schedule to have time to train. I was fortunate to have trained in NZ before so I knew the best places to go for swimming, biking and running.

I left London in winter and arrived in New Zealand in summer. I took my bike to a bike shop to be lubed and reassembled after being in a bike box on the plane.

The greatest challenge I noticed was the weather and time zone changes between the two countries. I had been training in close to zero degree temperatures and dull rainy days in London; now I was in hot and sunny conditions in NZ. I reversed my body clock completely. Training at 11.00 a.m. in NZ was actually 11.00 p.m. in London.

I packed summer training kit to take to NZ and made sure I started training slowly. In hot conditions I trained faster and harder which is enjoyable but at the same time dangerous in terms of injuries. I was sweating more and needed to hydrate carefully. I liked to stretch after my sessions to release the lactic acid build-up.

I came back to London better off from my training in NZ. I had successfully continued my training plan while abroad and actually had nicer conditions in which to do so. Be prepared to train when abroad and take care of your body. Travelling on planes and in different countries does change the pressure on your body. Avoid injuries at all cost.

TIPS

1. *Train the way you will race your Ironman e.g. clothing, race pace, nutrition*

2. *Build a flexible and positive mental attitude to overcome adversity in training and on race day*

3. *Learn to train when travelling*

CHAPTER EIGHT

The athletic body

At the elite level the Ironman's body is typically lean and slender. The lighter you are, the faster you can move. Over one year of training the first-time, Ironman's body will undergo a spectacular transformation. Standing at the Ironman start line you will look fit, healthy and toned.

When I began training for the Ironman I had been doing light weights in the gym twice a week. I have an athletic build with a light frame. Over one year of training my fat percentage dropped to 10%.

I saw an elite level nutritionist who advised me to eat six times a day with lots of vegetables and a good balance of proteins and carbohydrates. He also wanted me to drink four litres of water a day to get my body accustomed to retaining water for the Ironman.

In reality I ate three times a day. I generally had a healthy diet so eating good food came naturally. My problem was having the time to buy and eat it and then eating enough of it. If I had more time to prepare food at night my meals were more regular and better quality. My lunches were not always the best quality but I ate healthy breakfasts and dinners.

I drank two to three litres of water a day; in summer I drank more. I also hydrated when I trained in the gym and had an electrolyte drink on the bike. Being well hydrated kept me mentally alert for work. If I was dehydrated I felt very tired and less effective in training.

Strength training in the gym added bulk to my legs. The long bike rides, running and even the swimming helped them grow even more. My upper body responded to weight training; swimming and biking in the same way. My chest, shoulders and triceps muscles were the major muscle groups to become defined.

My clothes became looser in the upper body as I got leaner. This gave me the appearance of being very thin; however, under the clothing my body looked muscular with athletic definition. My new body shape was obvious when wearing my triathlon kit.

People commented on my healthy skin. The consistent aerobic training created a glow to my face. These benefits were highlighted even more with fat loss and muscular toning around my neck and shoulders.

I did not look great all the time and on days when I was tired and hungry I looked gaunt in the face. I lost the fullness around my cheekbones and my neck got thinner. People did worry I was getting too thin but this was a temporary phase during my biggest weeks of training combined with working very long hours.

Despite looking too thin at times and being tired, I could tell my body was getting race fit. It felt light, fast and strong. I was able to train for hours without fatigue. When I was extremely tired it was important for me to rest and eat well and then I would look healthy again.

On race day I was feeling super-fit and my body looked like I had trained for a full year. I had lost three to four kilos of fat and increased my muscle bulk. I felt light and ready to race fast. It was good to have some fat on my body for warmth; it also provided me with steady energy for 13 hours of continuous exercise. I was the fittest I had ever been in my life and it was an incredible feeling (see photos on www. physical-edge.com).

Story

The reality of tiredness

When I was Ironman training my body had to adapt to swimming, biking and running six times a week. The volume of training increased each successive week and I could feel my leg muscles ache and tighten more and more. The morning after intense or long training sessions my whole body hurt. Getting out of bed early in the morning was exhausting. It was tiring even lifting my arm up off the bed and sometimes I wondered how I was going to get through the rest of the day.

My body felt better mid-morning and by lunchtime I felt full of energy again and the tiredness in my body was gone. If I missed eating breakfast I was starving by lunchtime and if I did not drink enough I felt tired.

If I trained in the morning before work I felt really tired by the end of the day. Sometimes I worked until 8.00 p.m. By 5.00 p.m. the tiredness really set in. The last three hours of work were a challenge for me to stay focused as it was physically demanding working as a physiotherapist and running my own business. Being hungry, thirsty and tired day after day required great stamina and determination.

Occasionally I fell asleep when talking to my girlfriend (now wife). I did not see her during the day so when I got home she wanted to talk. She deserved lots of attention but I kept falling asleep mid-conversation. Sometimes I spoke total nonsense and we had a good laugh.

Fitness

My fitness in the Ironman improved with each long training session I completed. These sessions pushed my body to new limits. I could tell I was getting fitter because I could train harder, go faster and had better endurance.

Story

Evidence

It was a fantastic feeling getting fitter. By the time I was swimming for one hour, biking for three and a half hours and running for two hours I was doing much more training than the average person.

My level of fitness became evident when bike riding with friends. One Sunday a friend asked me to ride with him to Windsor Castle. I told him my strict training plan and it was important for me to stay at my race pace. He agreed to ride at my pace.

I dropped down into aero position and increased my speed to race pace. I kept a consistent cadence. My friend rode closely behind my bike. We climbed several hills and I maintained my race pace.

After two hours I looked back to see how my friend was going and he had fallen behind; I stopped and waited for him to catch up. He was surprised at my strength riding up hills and said he was struggling to keep up with me. At this point I knew I was getting much fitter.

TIPS

1. *Stick to the training programme and you will look athletic and lean*
2. *Physical tiredness is part of Ironman training so plan quality rest*
3. *Take small steps forwards in fitness and enjoy the incredible results*

Taking swim cap off for fast transition out of Lake Zurich

Half way through the bike leg of the Ironman

■   *'High 5's' to my support team*

▨ *Euphoric as I finish the marathon*

Wet suit on and ready to race, Bruce Scott with Rhys

Excited to start with my support team around me, Monique Scott with Rhys

My support team at the Ironman. Front left to right: Laura, Rhys, Monique, Michelle, Fran (Coach).
Back Left to right: Debbie, Joel, Tony, Bruce Scott, Bruce Goldfinch.

CHAPTER NINE

Healthy training

I was fortunate not to get sick once during my year of Ironman training. I was highly motivated to do everything right. I stayed away from other people who were sick and I had an annual medical examination and flu injection. I got fitter and my body got stronger and healthier.

The Ironman is a serious race. You cannot turn up to the start line, like a marathon, and get through it on guts and determination alone. It requires six months to a year of training. In this time the body is stressed to the limit; if it is not cared for injuries can occur.

Training with injuries

An Ironman wants to avoid injuries because they upset training and create setbacks in performance. Injuries can be a source of great anxiety, frustration and disappointment.

The secret to managing an injury is to do everything possible to heal it and, at the same time, continue to train without making the injury worse and maintain fitness levels.

A coach can help with training alterations and emotional support after an injury. A coach can put the injury back into a balanced perspective for the Ironman and decide on new training goals.

Story

Coach a lifesaver

I developed my training slowly one year before my Ironman race. Having a year to train gave me the time to make mistakes, get injured and recover. The distances I trained got gradually longer and I quickly progressed to training six days a week.

I was six weeks into my training when I felt my calf muscles get extremely tight. In the mornings the stiffness made it awkward to walk normally; to walk downstairs I had to go sideways. I had been training six days a week with one day's rest. I was sweating a lot and losing valuable salts from my body. I was not replacing the salts fast enough and my muscles responded by getting tighter.

One Sunday I had finished a two and a half hour bike ride and was in a rush to leave the house to catch up with friends. There were several flights of stairs in the house and in my haste to get ready I sprinted up them.

As I started the second flight of stairs I felt a sudden pulling pain on the inside of my left ankle. I stopped immediately and waited anxiously to see if it would go away. It settled when I was standing still but then hurt again each time I put pressure through my foot. In my mind it was a disaster, a stupid mistake because I was in a rush. I iced it immediately and then went out.

The next day I tried to cycle and the ankle was too painful. I even tried to swim and the action of kicking aggravated it. It was so frustrating knowing I had created this injury. The thought of losing valuable training time and fitness made me angry.

I called my coach in desperation for his advice. He listened empathetically and we assessed the situation together. My calf muscles had been very tight after the bike ride. The sudden change in action of running up the stairs strained a tendon in my ankle.

He reminded me of the benefits of training over a year. We had time to manage this injury and from a long-term perspective my training was not affected. He was always positive and optimistic when he spoke to me. He gave me clear instructions on what to change in training and what was important to maximise my recovery.

Within three weeks I was back to training. The injury needed rest and physiotherapy. My training changed to swimming using a buoy between my legs, and gym training. I had massage and stretched over foam rollers. When I started training again I felt a great relief. I learnt to be careful with my body to avoid another injury.

This experience made me appreciate even more the value of having a coach. I was able to offload my anxiety and fears on to him immediately and he helped me get a balanced view of what the injury meant to my training. His calmness and reassurance was just as important as the advice he gave me to manage the injury. When I compare using a computer program for a training programme and having a coach, I believe having a coach wins every time.

Nutrition

Getting over cramp

I suffered severe muscle cramping and tightness because I was losing too many salts from my body, sweating during training, and I was not replacing them. I took a close look at my nutrition to help.

I was in New Zealand and spoke to a medical practitioner who had helped endurance athletes with muscle cramp. He recommended a salt replacement taken from Lake Utah, USA. The key ingredients were magnesium and calcium and I took this twice a day. I poured 12 drops of concentrated salts into a glass of fruit juice and drank it; it had no taste so was pleasant to drink. The tightness in my legs eased and my muscle cramping stopped. It had a better effect than massage alone and in the mornings I felt freer to move.

I continued to use a salt replacement and also sought advice from other health professionals to enhance my recovery and performance through nutrition. I went for a men's health medical screening with a doctor, halfway through my training. The clinic I chose recommended natural forms of medicine before synthetic medicine when appropriate. I found the assessment was excellent because the doctor listened to what I was doing and could link his findings with my complaints. I told him I was doing an Ironman and he decided to give me a blood test.

The blood test results showed elevated levels of Creatine Kinase (CK). CK is an enzyme present in the blood when muscle tissue is broken down. The impact of running and long bike rides had been traumatising my muscle tissue and producing elevated levels of CK in my blood. It is normal for muscle tissue to break down when training as it then repairs stronger. The doctor recommended I take an antioxidant to help my body recover from muscle damage.

Antioxidants fight free radicals. Free radicals are produced not only through exercise but also pollution, stress, poor nutrition and even breathing. Free radicals destroy cells by stealing an electron from them. These electron-deprived cells then die. Millions of healthy cells are killed each day and my training was magnifying this effect.

My body was wasting valuable energy trying to recover from free radical invasion. If I took an antioxidant it would provide an electron to the free radicals so they did not destroy healthy cells with them. This made sense to me so I went looking for a high quality antioxidant.

The antioxidant product I chose to drink was Monavie. It contained 19 fruits of which the most powerful antioxidant was the Acai Berry. The Acai Berry was freeze-dried in the bottle to retain over 95% of its nutritional value and it tasted great. I took one-third of a wineglass morning and night to get maximum results (see www.physical-edge.com to find this product). I enjoyed taking Monavie so much I still take it today.

I continued to fine tune my nutrition and discovered the importance of blood pH on performance from Anthony Robbins and the Energise for Life website. Our cells function best when at a pH of 7.365. Our stressful lives, the environment and what we eat can create an acidity in our blood i.e. pH7 and below. Usually the body can buffer fluctuations in acidity but if we lose this buffer then cells start to break down and physical performance drops.

I measured my blood pH using saliva test strips and it was pH6. My excessive training had depleted my body of alkaline stores and now my body was very acidic. To rebalance my alkaline stores I drank two to four litres of water with alkalising greens and pH drops in it. These products raised the pH of the water to pH9. I was now drinking alkaline water and this helped restore my body's buffer zone for acid attacks. I also ate more green vegetables and salads because these also alkalised my body.

After two weeks of alkalising my body I measured my blood pH to see if there was any difference. It had risen to pH7-7.4 which was ideal. I knew the cells in my body were now in a healthy environment and were supported to function at their best. I got used to tasting alkaline water and I could feel my body was enjoying the change.

I took two other supplements to provide my body with nutrients possibly missing from my diet. These included a multivitamin and an Omega-3, -6 and -9 oil. The body cannot synthesise these products by itself and is reliant on nutrition to provide them. The food we buy from supermarkets is not high quality and my inconsistent meals meant I was possibly at risk of lacking these products. My doctor also said my skin was very dry because I was missing Omega oils in my diet. I took a multivitamin tablet and spoon of Omega oils once a day.

By assessing my nutrition and getting it right for my body I felt much healthier. I could recover faster and my performance vastly improved. It is important to test the products you buy on your own body and choose the most effective ones. Then be consistent at taking them and notice how good your body feels.

Story

Super power

I received an email from my homeopath and she recommended a sports supplement from a company called Mannatech. The directions were to drink it 30 minutes before I trained and 20 minutes after finishing training. I decided to try it on a Sunday long bike ride.

I drank it and felt more alert as I got ready for my bike ride. During the bike ride I was much stronger hill climbing and my endurance was drastically better. I was able to accelerate quickly and I could feel more power in my legs. I noticed I had loads of energy for the end of the bike ride. I wondered if it was an illegal drug but I was assured it had passed food standard authority tests.

There are many products like this on the market and I experimented with Mannatech and can recommend its effects. Remember always to test these products in training and never on race day.

TIPS

1. *Seek advice from a quality physiotherapist and your coach as soon as an injury occurs*
2. *Cramp can be helped with a high concentration magnesium and calcium product*
3. *Get your food supplementation right for your own body and test it in training*

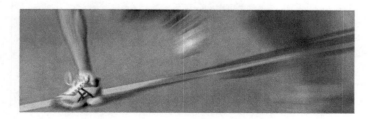

CHAPTER TEN

Equipment and technology for an Ironman

An Ironman is the greatest physical challenge in the sport of triathlon. The kit required to train and race an Ironman is highly specialised. It must withstand many hours of training and also a complete Ironman race. The kit must also look cool because Ironman athletes will admit to being quite vain. The cost of equipment can exceed hundreds if not thousands of pounds; generally you pay more for better quality equipment. To complete an Ironman you can use mid-range kit and equipment with confidence.

Story

Having the wrong equipment

When I started Ironman training it was summer and I was wearing summer gloves for bike riding. The season eventually changed to autumn and then winter but I was still wearing summer gloves. I went for a one hour ride around Richmond Park and noticed my fingers were getting cold. At first I thought this was normal for riding in cold weather and hoped they would warm up as the rest of my body warmed up.

After 10 minutes of riding, the tips of my fingers were even colder so I tried curling them into a fist to keep them warm. However, as I rode down hills in the park the wind chill increased and the temperature plummeted to sub-zero. The cold in my fingers got worse and then turned to pain. The pain escalated with every hill descent and my efforts to be strong and withstand it wilted away; eventually I had to stop because the pain was unbearable. I tucked my fingers under my armpits to warm them up. It took 10 minutes for the pain to subside and it was a great relief when my fingers felt normal again. I decided it was too cold to continue riding and returned home.

The next week I put on two pairs of gloves, with the outer pair being ski gloves. I rode around Richmond Park again and this time my fingers stayed warm. The ski gloves were effective but very bulky and made changing gears and braking difficult. I did not understand why other riders were not having the same problems.

I looked closer at the gloves other riders were wearing and noticed they were padded but much thinner.

I went home and searched the internet for winter biking gloves and found specialised gloves for sub-zero degree temperatures. They were designed for warmth and were thinner for safe control of the bike i.e. braking and gear changing. I felt such a 'mug' riding around Richmond Park in ski gloves.

I realised there was an entire range of clothing for bike riding in winter. I bought a bike jacket, it was a brand called 'Radiation' and had a silver lining inside for increased warmth. It was perfect for allowing perspiration to escape whilst being waterproof and windproof. My Radiation jacket was my favourite piece of winter clothing and proved priceless on wet and cold London mornings.

Swimming kit

Swimming requires a good pair of goggles and a quality wetsuit. I tried five pairs of goggles before finding two pairs I liked. I had a pair of goggles for bright and dark weather conditions. Goggles need to feel comfortable and be watertight. If goggles leak water during the race it can make life hellish; in fact, I would not finish a 3.8k swim with water-filled goggles.

Buying a wetsuit is the second biggest investment in Ironman after a bike. Today wetsuits are scientifically tested to speed up swimming times in triathlons. I bought a £350 wetsuit which was on sale for £150 in a triathlon store. It had ribbing on the forearms to create more friction as I pulled my arms through the water. The chest area was thicker for increased buoyancy and it fitted my body like a glove. The shoulders were made of a thinner material to allow freedom of movement and reduce fatigue.

Other wetsuits in the market have additional air cells around the thighs to keep heavy legs afloat. They can also have small fins on the forearms to generate further forward propulsion. The technology is astounding and you pay for it as some wetsuits can cost £500-£700.

Story

Tearing my wetsuit

I trained through winter in an indoor swimming pool. As soon as I was able to train outdoors I started using my new wetsuit which gave me extra buoyancy in the water. I noticed my shoulders felt free to move. I swam for 45 minutes much faster and easier than normal. The wetsuit reduced the drag on my body because it kept my body more horizontal in the water.

My wetsuit fitted my body like a glove; it was so tight I had trouble getting it on sometimes. One hot summer's day I heard a ripping sound as I was putting it on. I looked down and on my right thigh was a four-centimetre tear. My fingernails had dug into the wetsuit as I pulled it up and had ripped it. I had torn through the air cells in the wetsuit and when I got into the swimming pool the wetsuit leg filled with water. I completed my swim and could feel the water moving in the wetsuit leg. I was worried I would have to buy a new wetsuit and went to the local triathlon store to find out.

In the triathlon store the sales assistant suggested I glue the tear together. I did not know this was possible so I paid for the glue and he did it for me. He applied glue to the tear and then held it firmly together for 30 minutes. I took the glued wetsuit to the pool to test it and it worked brilliantly. The water had drained from the wetsuit leg and the tear no longer leaked. I was glad I saved £300 to £500 buying a new wetsuit.

I learnt to put my wetsuit on using body glide and plastic bags. Body glide covered my skin so the wetsuit could glide over it. The plastic bags covered my hands and feet so they could slip through the small openings in the arms and legs of the wetsuit easily. I also gripped the outside of the wetsuit with the pad of my thumb against the mid-section of each finger to avoid fingernail tears.

Story

Friction in neck

A problem I suffered all season was a rubbing of the wetsuit against the back of my neck and the creation of blisters. The blisters never healed properly because they were constantly irritated each time I went for a swim. To allow the blisters to heal and protect them I applied waterproof dressings over the top of them and applied body glide. This worked for one kilometre of swimming and then the dressings fell off. I discovered the solution during my Ironman race.

In the Ironman I wore my triathlon suit under my wetsuit; I did not do this in training. The collar of the suit covered my neck and when I finished the swim in the Ironman I did not have any blisters. Having a material layer between my skin and the wetsuit created a protective layer against blistering. It was a great discovery just at the right time.

Story

Wetsuit or no wetsuit swim

I had trained well in my wetsuit and was ready to use it for the Ironman. It saved me enormous amounts of energy when I swam which was key to my race plan.

Two days before the Ironman, the race officials tested the temperature of the water in Lake Zurich and it was 24.3 degrees Celsius. If the temperature exceeded 24.5 degrees Celsius wetsuits were banned for the race. At temperatures of 24.5 degrees or above there is greater risk of heat exhaustion when wearing wetsuits. The prospect of swimming without a wetsuit frightened me and most of the other Ironman athletes felt the same way. Eighty per cent of the Ironman entrants were first-timers and we all waited in anxious anticipation for the race officials to make a last-minute decision.

Race officials announced the water temperature one hour before the race started and then the ruling for wetsuits in the race. I tried to blank the thought of swimming without my wetsuit from my mind. I was prepared to do whatever it took to get through the swim.

Race officials finally announced a water temperature of 23 degrees, so wetsuits could be worn in the race. The entire Ironman field cheered. It was a real confidence booster to be wearing our wetsuits.

Biking kit

Buying a race bike is the greatest expense for an Ironman. The price can range from £600 to £10,000. If you are clear on your budget, riding experience and future plans, choosing the bike is much easier. I bought a bike costing £1,500. It was excellent quality and I raced the Ironman on it comfortably.

Story

Getting the right fit

I went to a triathlon store to choose my racing bike. I wanted to compete in road cycling after Ironman so I decided to buy a road bike. I converted the road bike to an Ironman bike by adding aero bars.

I had three bike fits before getting my bike feeling comfortable in aero position. I had the pressure through my feet assessed to make sure they were even on both sides as I peddled. I was fitted with wedges under my cleats to improve peddling pressure. My bike was also fitted with an adjustable metal joint connecting the handlebars to the bike's stem. It raised my body position upwards and backwards to relieve pressure in my back and neck.

I enjoyed using my bike even though it took several bike fits to get it comfortable. In hindsight, if I bought a road bike again I would purchase a made-to-measure frame. Normally, bike shops sell frames in a standard number of sizes; they then make adjustments to fit the rider to the bike as best they can. Made-to-measure frames are made from scratch to fit the rider's exact measurements.

Made-to-measure bikes can cost £7,000 or more. If this was within my budget and I bought one I believe my comfort on bike rides would be even better. It is the ultimate ride for those who want it and can afford it. I would avoid having additional attachments to the bike to make it fit; these attachments often destabilise a bike and can make riding dangerous.

The best time to buy a new bike is at the end of the summer season when triathlons have finished. Prices can drop by 50% as bike shops have sales to make space for new season stock. You can even ask for free extras if you are buying an expensive bike.

Bike wheels

If there is one piece of equipment to help improve bike speed in triathlon it is the wheels. Zipp wheels are the best on the market: they are super-light, aerodynamic and have been clinically tested to improve speed. A set of wheels can cost £1,500 and they are a luxury item to own.

Story

Faster than ever

I wanted to use Zipp wheels in the Ironman but I could not afford to buy them. In the last few months of training I befriended a triathlete who offered to lend me his Zipp wheels.

Two weeks before my race I put them on my bike and trained. The wheels were much lighter to ride on and my average speed increased by two to three kilometres an hour. My legs were stronger by this stage in training and having the Zipp wheels meant I was riding faster than I had ever ridden before.

In the Ironman I rode for six and a half hours and it was a hilly course. The Zipp wheels made a significant difference because they were light and I expended less energy in my legs. The bike felt easier to turn and faster to hill climb. When I transitioned from bike to run my legs took 10 kilometres to adjust to a change in motion but had plenty of energy to attack the marathon. I highly recommend Zipp wheels if you can afford them.

Running kit

Wearing correct running shoes can reduce the chances of injury. Every year new shoes are developed by sports companies to control how the foot impacts the ground in running. The choice of shoe you buy will depend on your anatomy and lower limb biomechanics as you run.

Story

How shoes help

I wanted a new pair of running shoes for Ironman training; the shoes had to support orthotics I already owned. I went to a running store in New Zealand and ran on a treadmill in several different pairs of shoes. The pair I bought appeared to fit well so I bought them. I realised later they created a blister when running longer distances but by this time I had already flown back to London. The shoes were too big and my heel rubbed against the heel cup.

I took the shoes to a running store in London to get help. The shop assistant looked at the shoes I had bought in New Zealand and recommended a much lighter, more flexible pair to try. I ran down the road to test them. They felt more supportive and instantly more comfortable. I decided to buy them and as I was desperate to get rid of the blisters I also bought 'blister free' socks. These socks were double-layered to reduce rubbing between the foot and the shoe.

I took my new shoes home and went for a 30 minute run to test them; I did not get any blisters. To test them again I ran for 45 minutes and still no blisters. It was a great relief to be running pain-free. It pays to get good advice and buy the correct running shoes from a reputable running store.

My coach advised me to buy two pairs of the same running shoes once I found a pair I liked. He predicted I would wear out one pair and need a second pair closer to Ironman. He was right and I was glad I followed his advice because the model I bought changed after eight months. If I used a new model shoe I was once again exposing myself to new injuries.

Other useful kit

Triathlon suit

The Ironman racing suit can come as a one or two-piece suit. Professionals wear one-piece suits but as an amateur I preferred the convenience of a two-piece suit. A two-piece suit allowed me to interchange tops and bottoms, especially when training six days a week and washing it. It is also less hassle when stopping for the toilet because I was able to leave the top on.

The two-piece suit consists of a sleeveless skin-tight racing vest and thigh-length racing shorts. My brother bought me a two-piece racing suit in New Zealand to support my Ironman challenge. Racing shorts have padding in the crotch to make bike riding more comfortable. When I inspected the chamois in the shorts my brother bought me it looked much thinner than normal. However, when I put them on they provided the right amount of protection for bike riding and were also comfortable to run in. In the race I used chamois cream to further reduce the chances of friction on the bike seat.

The racing top is skin-tight to allow total freedom of movement in the body and arms. There are pockets on the back for carrying essentials like food, air canisters and phone. It is designed to reduce wind resistance, keep the Ironman cool and it dries very quickly after swimming because it is made of thin, aerated, synthetic material.

I wore my racing suit under my wetsuit during the swim leg of the Ironman. It stayed on as I transitioned on to the bike and then into the run. Wearing it for the entire race is a time-saving strategy and one less thing to think about.

Story

Breaking the rules

In the Switzerland Ironman it was illegal to urinate on the side of the road. If we broke the rules we risked disqualification. The only place where toilets were available happened to be at aid stations. There were only six aid stations for each 90 kilometre loop of the bike leg in the Ironman.

Exiting Lake Zurich after the 3.8km swim, I suffered bad stomach cramps. The first 40 kilometres of the bike leg were completed in pain. I actually wanted to urinate but there were no toilets nearby. The urgency to urinate grew stronger and so did the stomach pain. I held on as long as I could but it was too painful and I decided to urinate. I did not want to get disqualified so I urinated whilst riding my bike. It was embarrassing at the time but I had no other option.

Urinating whilst riding my bike was not something I had practised in training. Naturally I stopped pedalling and relaxed to go. The urine collected in one short leg and then exploded out as the pressure of it overcame the elastic band in the shorts around my thigh. It was the only time I was grateful for the 'no drafting' rule in Ironman; the cyclist behind could avoid the spray. I poured water over my shorts to clean myself when I finished.

Once I had urinated I felt significantly better and my stomach pain disappeared. I was able to ride faster without pain. It made such a big difference and I urinated on my bike when I felt the urge for the rest of the race.

Heart rate monitor

I used a heart rate monitor to measure the intensity of my training sessions and monitor my progress during Ironman. My maximum heart rate was 170 beats per minute (BPM) and my resting heart rate was 33 BPM. I was professionally tested to find my maximum and resting heart rates. The tests included running on a treadmill until complete exhaustion and sitting still for 10 minutes whilst recording my heart rate.

When I started Ironman training my comfortable training heart rate was 120-135 BPM. I could sustain this for long hours of training. As I got fitter I noticed 135-145 BPM became my new comfort zone. At higher fitness levels I could race faster for longer and recover quicker.

My coach also used heart rates to improve my aerobic fitness. He set the heart rate zones for my long bike rides and runs. Sometimes it was 65-70% of maximum heart rate and other times it was 85-95% of maximum heart rate. One training session may have combined several heart rate zones. Generally, the higher the heart rate zone in training, the shorter the length of the training session e.g. running at 80-90% of maximum heart rate for 45 minutes or bike riding at 65-70% of maximum heart rate for six hours.

After training with my heart rate monitor for six months I could feel what different heart rates felt like in my body. If I was training at high intensity heart rates I knew what the strain felt like on my body and vice versa for low intensity heart rates. In the Ironman I did not wear my heart rate monitor and successfully paced my race based on feeling alone.

Story

The Beast

The Switzerland Ironman is different from other Ironman races because the bike leg is mountainous. The biggest mountain to climb is called The Beast.

The bike leg consisted of a 90 kilometre lap done twice. During the first lap I felt strong and overtook groups of riders along the way. I approached The Beast and suddenly my heart rate rocketed. My speed slowed to a snail's pace. I looked up at the turns ahead and they disappeared into the distance. It was a real grind to the top. I could hear music from a band playing at the summit of the mountain. My thigh muscles were burning and my breathing was laboured. I kept a steady speed and made it to the summit. I realised 'The Beast' was an appropriate name for the mountain. After passing the summit I rested as I coasted down the mountain for five minutes.

The Beast was a tough climb and it exhausted my leg muscles. I knew I had to climb it again so slowed down during the second lap to conserve energy for the marathon to come. I completed the first lap 30 minutes faster than the second lap. I controlled my heart rate better in the second lap and started the marathon feeling good.

Garmin bike computer

I bought a Garmin bike computer. I used the Garmin to track my rides with GPS and measure heart rate, cadence and time. It detected when I stopped riding and started again. The battery lasted longer than six and a half hours and it was fully waterproof. I took it overseas to train because it used satellite technology.

I would recommend the Garmin computer but it can be complicated to set up and is expensive to buy. If you do not need to track your rides by GPS then a standard speed and cadence reader on your bike is enough. I would monitor my heart rate using my Ironman watch.

TIPS

1. *Buy good quality training kit for each season of the year*

2. *Learn what works from other Ironman athletes*

3. *Don't buy gadgets you don't need i.e. stick to basics*

CHAPTER ELEVEN

Friends, family and supporting a charity

Ironman training is usually a solitary exercise because a training programme is specifically designed for one person. It does not take long to get used to training alone but on race day it is a great advantage to have your friends and family present with you. It is also empowering to raise money for a charity you support. Supporting a charity reminds you there is something greater than yourself to think about on race day.

Give to a charity

I chose to race my Ironman for a charity called KIVA. KIVA provides entrepreneurs in poor countries with microfinance to start their own businesses. Its website lists entrepreneurs: their businesses, lives and dreams and includes photographs of each of them. You choose which entrepreneur you want to support and loan them money.

Each entrepreneur pays back the loaned money with interest. Paying back the loan with interest teaches the entrepreneur how to manage cash flow and debt. Once the loan is repaid the money is loaned again to another entrepreneur. The money is continuously recycled to support more and more people. KIVA raises standards of living for the entrepreneur and his/her family and also the immediate community through the creation of jobs and providing new services. I raised $2,500 and loaned money to over 15 different entrepreneurs. I show on my website (www.physical-edge.com see Charity) who the money is loaned to, when it is paid back and the next entrepreneur to whom it is loaned.

People wanted to donate money to KIVA because they could not believe how long an Ironman race was in distance or time. They were excited by the challenge and naturally wanted to be part of it. After donating money they felt invested in the challenge and followed my progress via my blog (www.physical-edge.com see Wordpress). I am very grateful to all my friends and family who donated so generously to KIVA. You have changed people's lives by doing so.

Supporters are amazing

I was fortunate to have nine people supporting me in Zurich for the Ironman. They included my girlfriend and her family (Laura, Tony, Debbie and Joel), friends from London (Bruce Scott, Monique, Bruce Goldfinch and Michelle) and my coach (Fran). They were amazing as they sacrificed their time and money to be there and made my experience at the Ironman an incredible one.

On race day they woke up at 5.00 a.m. to be with me at the start line. They cheered all day with pompoms and placards of support. Some of the placards read, 'Go Rhys! Keep going Rhys! Looking good Rhys!' My immediate family could not be with me in Zurich so my supporters surprised me with their messages of support on placards as well. I could recognise my supporters because they were waving a New Zealand (NZ) flag, had NZ stickers on their faces and arms and were the noisiest people on the course. I provided them with white Physical Edge T-shirts and hats which made it easy to spot them from a distance.

In the marathon I could hear them before I saw them and they 'high fived' me as I ran past.

I looked forward to seeing them each time I completed a 10 kilometre lap. Their cheering raised my spirits. I could not imagine running the marathon without supporters. I remember hearing them scream, "See you at the finish line!" as I ran past them the final time. It was a special moment to share the Ironman with them all.

My team of supporters also cheered for other Ironman athletes on the course. They developed a friendship with an Englishman named Paul who had a great sense of humour. Every time Paul ran past they gave him loads of encouragement. Paul bantered back and it kept him going in the marathon all the way to the finish line. Once he crossed the finish line and recovered, the team asked to have a photo taken with him. He was so appreciative of everyone's support he wanted to take a photo home himself.

A few weeks after the Ironman I got an email from Paul. He remembered the Physical Edge logo on the front of everyone's white T-shirts and found my business website and blog. He wrote: 'Thanks to everyone who was out on the run course shouting for us poor fools who were running the final few miles. It was an incredible experience, one which I shall enjoy the memories of for a VERY long time to come.' An Ironman is a race to remember for the rest of your life. Supporters are a big part of that memory as they bring so much emotion to the experience; they are the life force of an action-packed day.

Story

My greatest supporter

Ironman training became the number one priority of my life. I ran my business during the day, trained and spent as much time as possible with my new girlfriend, Laura.

When I first met Laura I was already training for the Ironman. I was reluctant to have a girlfriend at the time but my coach said it was important to have a close personal relationship when doing an Ironman. We spent more and more time together but as my training increased I warned her about my tiredness, mood swings and desire for early nights. She wanted to make the relationship last so we continued to see each other.

Training gradually took over more of my time, which meant sacrificing time with Laura.

When we were together I was often physically exhausted from training. I tried to give her my fullest attention but I had difficulty concentrating. Once I remember falling asleep in mid-conversation and waking up thinking I was in a dream. I could hear Laura talking but had not heard a word she had said. Laura laughed when I answered a question I had heard in my dream on a totally unrelated subject. I often drifted in and out of consciousness in our late night conversations.

Laura worked as a professional musician for a London-based orchestra and performed in a band at weddings. She worked in the evenings and on weekends. Her schedule coincided nicely with Ironman training. When she was working in the evening or sleeping late in the morning I could train; after training I spent the rest of the day with her.

Laura supported me emotionally throughout my training and generally made life easier. She made me dinner at night and I looked forward to seeing her at the end of my long days.

On the day of the Ironman she flew to Zurich at 4.00 a.m. She had performed the night before and only had two hours' sleep. She arrived at the race in time to see me transition from the swim on to my bike. I loved seeing her smiling face as I cycled past. She cheered all day. During the marathon I grabbed her hand as I saw her close up for the first time. She lip-synced 'I love you' and blew me a kiss. She was my greatest supporter.

In the final 200 metres of the marathon I thought about Laura and my plan to propose marriage to her in four days' time in Santorini, a Greek Island. I had been organising the proposal for three months and it was a surprise; the proposal was going to change our lives forever and I was excited. It was an emotional last 200 metres and I treasured every step to the finish line.

After crossing the finish line I was directed to the recovery tent where I ate food and found a thermal blanket. All I wanted to do was see my supporters and give Laura a hug and kiss. Laura had accompanied me along my entire Ironman journey and it is a memory we will always have together for the rest of our lives.

Story

Overseas supporters

My family and friends who could not come to Zurich to see me race wanted to follow my progress on the day. I directed them to a website called ironmanlive.com. On this website my times were displayed for each transition and at several key points in the marathon. Those who logged on could watch me progress through the race and know when I finished in real time.

Ironmanlive.com tracked me during the race using an electronic chip around my ankle. When I crossed recording mats the website displayed my time.

In the marathon the website recorded my time splits over four laps of the course. I completed the first lap in 1.06.35 hours and the second lap in 1.15.19 hours. Everyone watching could feel my pain as I began to slow down. I completed my final two laps in 1.16.53 hours and 1.21.04 hours. It was agonising to watch and a relief for everyone when I crossed the finish line.

TIPS

1. *Maintaining a personal relationship during Ironman is important*

2. *Bring as many friends and family to support you at the Ironman and race for charity*

3. *Make the day fun for everyone*

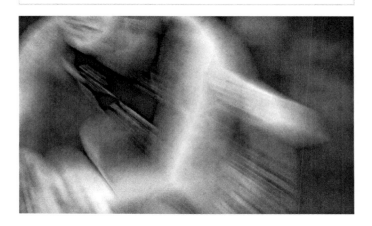

CHAPTER TWELVE

The Ironman race

My business website had a countdown clock on its home page showing the number of days to go to the Ironman. When I entered the Ironman it displayed 365 days, the race seemed too far away to be real.

My training went well, and with so much to learn the months counted down quickly. Before I knew it, a year had almost passed and the Ironman was only two weeks away. It was time to start tapering (reduce the volume of training) and prepare psychologically for the race.

Psychologically, I wanted to have fun in the race, enjoy the experience and absorb the atmosphere. I went to my mental conditioning coach to work on a visualisation for race day.

The visualisation was one hour long and created the entire race in my head. It began at breakfast and included details like the landscape of the bike course, what I would say to myself when the going was tough and how I wanted to finish the race. I relived my celebration as I crossed the finish line and thanked my supporters at the end. I listened to my visualisation many times, as it was recorded on my iPod. The mental imagery on the recording was the key to my confidence before and during my Ironman race. I was able to relax, stay calm and enjoy every moment of it.

My coach travelled with me to Zurich and we had two days before the race to get prepared. When we arrived it was raining heavily but the weather forecast was a sunny day for the race. I organised my Ironman kit and went to Ironman Village to register. My coach made sure I kept eating every three to four hours and sipping electrolyte and water all day. He had actually raced the Switzerland Ironman before and knew exactly what to do. It was reassuring to have him with me and we joked a lot to keep my mood upbeat and positive.

I bought last-minute supplies from Ironman Village and racked my bike in the transition zone. It was still raining heavily the day before the Ironman but the Swiss race officials were adamant the weather would change. As it turned out they predicted correctly and everything was set for a fantastic day of racing.

It was the day of the Ironman. I woke up at 5.00 a.m. to have breakfast; I then caught a tram to Ironman Village. At 6.30 a.m. I was sitting on a bench at the gates to the start line, looking directly over Lake Zurich. My supporters were around me and there was an exciting buzz in the air. In less than one hour's time I was about to start the Ironman.

Lake Zurich looked calm with no wind and it was slightly overcast in the sky. The race conditions were perfect and I could feel energy inside my body wanting to burst out. The moment was incredible and it felt surreal after 12 months of training.

Fifty minutes passed and I was now standing in the sand on the banks of Lake Zurich, waiting for the 10-second countdown to begin. The 2,222 Ironman athletes were nervous but raring to go. Everyone looked fit in their wetsuits and were circling their arms in the air to warm up. The professional athletes started five minutes before everyone else. We watched them swim towards the first marker with the morning sun rising ahead of them. The marker looked far away; we all clapped as they swam off into the distance.

The race official instructed us to enter the water and approach the start line. The start line was a yellow rope running between two floats 10 metres offshore. The countdown began: 10, 9, 8, 7, 6, 5, 4, 3, 2 ...1. Suddenly cowbells rang loudly above our heads to announce the official start of the Ironman.

I wanted to avoid the mad scramble of swimmers at the front of the race pack so kept to the back and side of everyone. I could feel water fill my wetsuit as I walked into deeper water and then I launched myself into full swimming stroke.

I started swimming and looked up to see where the first marker was positioned. I wanted a landmark to swim towards. I decided to wear clear goggles that morning because the sky looked overcast. Five minutes into the swim and the sun was sitting higher in the sky; it shone through the cloud cover and directly into my eyes. I could only see two metres ahead and the first marker was impossible to sight. The lake was dark and murky so I had very little navigation under the water as well. I followed the swimmers in front of me, hoping they were going the right way. I felt tired swimming the first 800 metres of the race. It did not help my confidence when swimmer after swimmer overtook me. At one stage I had a race official sitting in an outboard boat next to me, shouting commands through a megaphone. I was not sure if his commands were directed at me or someone else but I wondered if I was one of the swimmers at the back of the entire field. Despite my confusion, I stuck to my pace and followed the swimmers ahead of me.

At the first marker everyone converged to follow the fastest line around it. I swam on top of another Ironman as he crossed my swimming line to the marker. It was a dogfight for space and energy-zapping. I rounded the marker and remembered my coach's instructions to draft another swimmer and conserve energy. It took me five minutes to find a swimmer going at the right pace and in the correct direction. I swam directly behind him and relaxed.

The rest of the swim was tiring as we swam round and then ran across a small island at the halfway point. I could feel my body weaken in the last 500 metres. All I wanted was to get on my bike and start riding. I exited the lake with heavy legs and stomach cramps. It took me four minutes to transition on to my bike as I took my time to recover.

I continued to suffer stomach cramps for the first 50 kilometres of the bike course. I desperately needed to urinate and when I finally did, the pain eased. I could ride much faster without stomach cramps but I paced myself carefully to conserve energy for the marathon ahead. With five kilometres to go I slowed down and spun (rotated) my legs faster to simulate a running cadence. I finished the bike course feeling tired but ready to run. I transitioned into my running shoes and set off on the run course. I knew this was the point the Ironman really started. It was the first time I had ever run a marathon and I was extra cautious pacing myself.

The marathon had been divided into four laps of just over 10 kilometres each. I focused on completing and counting down one lap at a time; it was easier to comprehend than 42 kilometres all at once. I got slower and slower with each completed lap and in the final lap I felt horrendous pain in my thighs. The pain felt like glass tearing my muscles apart. I wanted to stop running but I was determined to finish without stopping. To motivate myself I focused on reaching each successive aid station and then the finish line.

I could hear spectators cheering as I got closer to the finish line. The race broadcaster was announcing the name of each Ironman running down the finishing ramp. I had 100 metres to run and I could not believe I was about to finish.

I ran towards the final turning point and pivoted 180 degrees on to the finishing ramp. I could see spectators standing behind advertising boards lining each side of the ramp. They were clapping and smacking the advertising boards with their hands for every Ironman finisher. As I looked around, I knew I had dreamed of this moment for a year. I was only seconds away from finishing the Ironman.

Twenty metres from the finish line I thrust my arms up to the heavens. I wanted to enjoy this moment with my entire body. I shook my head uncontrollably from side to side and cried, "Yeeeeeeeeeeeeeeesss!" with all the energy I had left. The crowds around me waved their hands for 'high fives'. Their smiles were as big as mine as I reached out with the full span of both arms to slap their hands as I ran past. I felt amazing as I recalled the training I had done to get to the finish line, including the long dark days, tiredness and the sacrifices I had made along the way. It was all worth it for this one euphoric moment.

As I crossed the finish line, I jumped into the air and spun 360 degrees. I looked up at the finishing clock and was surprised to see 12.55 hours. I had not looked at my watch for the entire race. It was a great time and better than I expected. I had become an Ironman at last. Volunteers put an Ironman medal round my neck and directed me to the recovery tent. I wrapped myself in a silver thermal blanket and sat down to eat chicken stew on rice. I was starving and the cooked food was just what I wanted; I did not want to eat another energy bar for a long time.

After eating I left the tent to look for my excited support team. They had made my race incredibly special and I wanted to enjoy it with them all. I saw my girlfriend first and she gave me a big hug and kiss. I looked forward to surprising her in four days' time with my marriage proposal. I turned to the rest of the Physical Edge support team and hugged and thanked each one of them individually. They made my race come to life. They were the energy pushing me to the finish line. They all hold a special place in my heart and I will remember their love and support for the rest of my life.

Fifteen minutes after finishing the race my legs were cramping. I needed help to walk and used my girlfriend's father's shoulder as a crutch. I hobbled to transition and collected my bike. It was time to head back to our hotels on the train. We decided to have a drink at my hotel before going our separate ways. Whilst there, my best friend told me he had proposed to his girlfriend the night before the race. It was a double celebration that night.

After drinks we went back to our hotel rooms for a happy night's sleep. My coach ran me a hot bath and my entire body relaxed as I soaked in it. Within five minutes I lowered my head in my hands, absolutely exhausted. I reflected on the day and what I had just achieved. It was one of the most rewarding experiences of my life.

After my bath I organised room service and enjoyed dinner with my girlfriend. She looked after me and eventually tucked me into bed at 11.00 p.m. My legs were burning from inflammation but my upper body was freezing from exhaustion. I covered my upper body with the duvet and drifted off to sleep. I woke a few times in the night from discomfort in my legs, but otherwise slept soundly until morning.

In the morning I was starving. My metabolism was at an all-time high and I could feel my muscles wasting away as we waited for breakfast. After breakfast I ate every two to three hours to satisfy my hunger pains. We spent the rest of the day relaxing in Zurich before catching a plane back to London the next day.

Two days after returning to London, my girlfriend and I flew to Santorini in the Greek Islands. I had planned a surprise holiday at an award-winning hotel called Kati Kies. I proposed to her on our first night. We were served dinner by our butler on the balcony of our room, surrounded by candles, overlooking the Caldera as the sun was setting. We celebrated our engagement with champagne. It was the perfect time to call family and friends to tell them our happy news. I was the happiest Ironman on the planet.

Post-Ironman

I returned to work after a romantic Greek Island holiday. It was extremely busy in the physiotherapy clinic and I was working 12-14 hours a days. I was not eating properly or getting enough sleep. My body was still recovering from the Ironman and I found concentrating difficult, as well as having a poor memory. It took me seven weeks to recover fully from the Ironman. In hindsight, I would have a longer break after the Ironman and rest more when back to work.

Despite feeling tired for seven weeks after the Ironman, my body actually wanted to train. Training had been ingrained in my body and was now an automatic desire. I spoke to my coach and he advised me to rest for six to eight weeks. It was the right advice as I can now look back and see how exhausted I actually had been.

Training for the Ironman gave me a physical challenge to focus on. I enjoyed the aerobic exercise and being outside pushing myself to the limit. I needed a new challenge to keep me motivated. I decided to enter the Etape Du Tour (stage of the Tour De France) the following year. I enjoyed cycling and wanted to take it to the next level. A 208 kilometre hilly course in the Massif Central of France was now awaiting me.

Memories

I have incredible memories of training for and racing the Ironman. It was an emotional experience: determination, pain, fun, laughter, excitement, satisfaction, disbelief, relief, success, love and euphoria. What I thought was impossible I dared to take on, and with faith and positive intention achieved a dream of a lifetime.

I went to see a picture framer to have my race number, medal, certificate and official photos framed. I realised there was one photo missing and went home to get it. I added a photo of all my supporters at the Ironman race. When I look at the finished framing it is the photo of my supporters I enjoy viewing the most as it brings back the most vivid memories of my race.

TIPS

1. *The hard training has been done, now the race is to enjoy*

2. *Be present in the Ironman and soak up the experience*

3. *Allow seven weeks to recover from the race and your body will thank you for it*

CHAPTER THIRTEEN

Life changes after Ironman

The Ironman has changed me in many ways because it constantly pushed me beyond my comfort zone and challenged me to grow in several areas of my life. I learned to always perform at my best and search to be better. I set higher standards in many areas of my life, including nutrition, exercise and goal-setting. I have a greater desire to experience success and I have zero tolerance for laziness. I like achieving outstanding results. I realise life is short and time is precious. If I want to do more in my life, I must get off my butt and do it. It is inspirational to know I can dream and make that dream a reality.

Since the Ironman I look after my nutrition and alkalise my body. I eat less processed food and red meat because it is acidic and requires enormous energy from the body to be digested. I strengthen my body against disease with an antioxidant (Monavie), Omega oils and multivitamins.

I value rest and I understand how good quality sleep is so important for peak performance.

If I get injured I get treatment immediately to prevent the consequences of stiffness and weakness affecting my physical performance. I also invest time in mental conditioning to make recovery from injury a positive experience. Mental conditioning has also carried over to my work and personal life where clarity of what I want has made a significant difference to what actually happens.

I believe in using coaches and choosing those who have already done what I want. I employ coaches for work and for anything else I want to learn fast. My coaches become friends and talking openly and honestly to them clears my mind to make better decisions for the future.

I have learned how I react under physical and mental stress and how to manage my life and emotions in empowering ways. I like goal-setting and having a clear plan of action. I get great satisfaction in being disciplined and taking small steps towards my goals. If my goals are exciting and desirable I can be doggedly determined to finish them and I enjoy seeing them completed.

I have become incredibly independent since the Ironman. Being responsible for my own training and racing created within me a 'Can Do' attitude. I am less patient and more direct with my language and actions. I have learned to trust my own instincts, use my own initiative and be accountable to my own high standards. I like making decisions and I have no time for people who complain or blame others before looking at themselves when things go wrong. If I make a mistake I take the lessons and aim to move forward.

All the learning I have taken from the Ironman has made my life richer. It has been one of the most powerful experiences of my life. If I think I cannot do something in my life it is begging for me to step up and do it. I suggest the Ironman is more than just a race.

Secrets to achieving goals

The Ironman was a daunting challenge but by completing it I have discovered my personal steps to achieving any goal I set in my life.

Once I have chosen what I want to do, the first step is to have faith and commit to it – commit to it in such a way that I cannot turn back. Pay a coach who has done what I want to do before and work together. Decide on other team members with complementary skills to further assist in achieving my goal. Select the appropriate team based on expertise and passion.

Get extreme clarity on each outcome necessary to achieve my goal and put timeframes with them. Create a final plan. Have the discipline and focus to follow through with the plan. Visualise achieving my goal like a movie, with sound and colour as if it was real life. Make sure I stay physically healthy to always perform at my best.

It is vital to have fun along the way and have family and friends involved in the process. Support a charity to create greater motivation and interest in what I am doing. Celebrate when the goal has been achieved and learn what I can do better next time. Finally, set a new goal before or as soon as the current goal has been achieved.

TIPS

1. *Learn from the Ironman how to live a healthy lifestyle*

2. *Take the secrets of your success in Ironman to other areas of your life*

3. *Be an inspiration to those around you*

CHAPTER FOURTEEN

You can do an Ironman with the right team behind you

Completing the Ironman has been the greatest physical challenge I have ever achieved in my life. I am proud to say I am an Ironman and want to share what I have learned with other people wanting to set a new standard in their life.

The journey is unforgettable and it will energise your life in more ways than you can ever imagine. It will be physically and mentally tough but you will get through it with the right support team behind you. You will develop new friendships along the way and you will take on adversity with a new determination to win. The race is amazing and you will have fun.

Anyone can do an Ironman if they have enough desire. The oldest person I have seen compete in an Ironman is 85 years old. I have seen a handicapped child pushed in his wheelchair by his father, a woman with an amputated leg and a 53-year-old man who is legally blind all finish. You can amaze yourself and be an Ironman too (check out stories of real Ironman athletes on www.physical-edge.com).

CHAPTER FIFTEEN

The opportunity

I am passionate about helping other people complete an Ironman for the first time. I have an Ironman Support Team ready to help you take on this challenge over one year. We have the experience and contacts in London to make your journey a major success.

If you are an entrepreneur, celebrity or businessman and want to take on an Ironman, we will take care of the logistics and training schedule for you. We can access equipment you need to buy and even organise your own personal assistant for easy coordination with your Ironman Support Team.

The Ironman Support Team is dedicated to your success and we want you to have an incredible experience. We know every journey is unique and we will work with you to create a truly bespoke service.

If you are ambitious and want to have an outstanding Ironman experience contact us on www.physical-edge.com

38-year-old New Zealand born Rhys Chong trained in his home country as a physiotherapist, qualifying in 1995 and completed a Post Graduate Diploma in Manipulative Physiotherapy 2 years later. In 1999, Rhys travelled to the UK for what was meant to be just two years, however has stayed ever since.

He worked in various private practices for two years before taking up a management and development position within a leading Physiotherapy business in London for five years. In this role Rhys taught two day Physiotherapy courses around the UK and Norway.

In 2008, Rhys set up his own Physiotherapy Practice in Fulham, London and moved to South Kensington, London in 2009 where he is still today.